WALKS IN RIBBLE COUNTRY

AN ILLUSTRATED GUIDE TO
THIRTY WALKS
'TWIXT RIBBLEHEAD AND LYTHAM

JACK KEIGHLEY

OLD WELL HALL, DOWNHAM

WALKS IN RIBBLE COUNTRY

AN ILLUSTRATED GUIDE TO THIRTY WALKS 'TWIXT RIBBLEHEAD AND LYTHAM

by

J Keighley

CICERONE

2 POLICE SQUARE, MILNTHORPE, CUMBRIA LA7 7PY
www.cicerone.co.uk

Also by *Keighley*

WALKS IN THE YORKSHIRE DALES
ISBN 1 85284 034 X

**WALKS IN THE YORKSHIRE DALES
BOOK TWO**
ISBN 1 85284 065 X

**WALKS IN THE YORKSHIRE DALES
BOOK THREE**
ISBN 1 85284 085 4

WALKS IN LANCASHIRE WITCH COUNTRY
ISBN 1 85284 093 5

WALKS ON THE NORTH YORK MOORS
ISBN 1 85284 134 6

**WALKS ON THE NORTH YORK MOORS
BOOK TWO**
ISBN 1 85284 197 4

**FAMILY WALKS IN THE
FOREST OF BOWLAND**
ISBN 1 85284 251 2

INTRODUCTION

High on the lonely, windswept, north-western flank of Cam Fell, in the Yorkshire Dales, there is a small, dark, limestone outcrop. A tiny, crystal-clear spring bubbles forth from its base, trickles falteringly down a grassy slope, then snakes invisibly through extensive beds of rushes to emerge as a purposeful rivulet carving its own little groove down the rough fellside. And purposeful it certainly needs to be for, though here known somewhat prosaically as Jam Sike, this is in fact the River Ribble setting off on its momentous 75-mile journey to the Irish Sea.

In its infancy the Ribble is flowing over boulder-clays deposited some 8,000 years ago by the glaciers of the last Ice Age. The moorland is dark and sombre, but there are soon signs of better things ahead, for at Thorns Gill the river has cut through into the underlying limestone to form a scenic little gorge. For the next 20 or so miles – as far as Settle – it is destined to pass through some of the most dramatic countryside in England.

'Three Peaks Country' is a veritable paradise for walkers, cavers and geologists. Determined peak-baggers and fitness-freaks arrive from far and wide to face the challenge of the magical trio – Whernside, Ingleborough and Penyghent. More leisurely ramblers may follow ancient green tracks over the hills, enjoying the dry, velvety turf of the limestone pastures and marvelling at the gleaming scars, spectacular ravines and gorges, fantastic pavement formations and boulder-strewn dry valleys. Intrepid potholers meanwhile will disappear down dank and sinister holes to crawl about in the Stygian gloom of labyrinthine cave systems.

Upon leaving the National Park our hitherto sprightly river undergoes a manifest personality-change as it meanders slowly through a flood plain which was once the bed of a vast, glacial ribbon-lake. These marshy meadows, known as 'Ings of Ribble' or 'Ribble Flats', attract few walkers but provide an ideal habitat for swans, geese and waders such as lapwing and redshank.

Approaching Paythorne the Ribble enters God's Own County, and Ribblesdale becomes the Ribble Valley. For many folk the image of Lancashire is one of dismal terraced streets in grimy mill towns, but the rambler in the Ribble Valley will discover a Lancashire rich in natural beauty and touched but lightly by the Industrial Revolution. The magnificent limestone gorge twixt Gisburn and Sawley forms the portal to the kind of idyllic countryside that you might have thought had gone for ever – rolling green hills, flowery meadows, shady woodlands and narrow, leafy lanes through picturesque villages that date back to pre-Conquest times. The area is steeped in fascinating history, and all along the Ribble's banks stand the hoary old halls and elegant mansions of illustrious Lancashire families.

The broad river slides sedately on, skirting the dire industrial sprawl of Preston to enter a strange, tide-washed world of saltmarshes, mud-flats and sandbanks, where huge flocks of wildfowl and waders may be seen feeding at low-tide. The Ribble Estuary is Britain's third most important for wading birds, and is designated as a National Nature Reserve.

The aim of this brief introduction is to convey a general impression of the superb countryside which the lucky user of this book may expect to enjoy. The walks have been selected to appeal to all tastes, and range from simple valley strolls to strenuous fell expeditions which may require navigational skills in the event of mist. Researching and recording these walks has given me enormous pleasure which I hope you will share as you follow in my footsteps.

J. Keighley

December 1998

5

SOME WORDS OF ADVICE

- Many of the routes in this book cross agricultural land, and farmers will not welcome inconsiderate visitors. When crossing fields keep closely to paths and walk in single file across meadowland. Avoid climbing walls, and securely close all gates behind you (unless they are obviously meant to be left open).

- Leave no litter.

- Cars must not be parked where they obstruct field gates or cause damage to grass verges. Lock your car and hide from view any attractive or valuable articles (or take them with you).

- Some of the walks described in this book cross high, exposed moorland terrain where the weather conditions may be less pleasant than at valley level. Should the weather turn nasty, don't hesitate to call it a day and return by the route along which you came.

- Before setting out, let others know exactly where you're going (especially if you're walking alone).

- When walking along a motor-road walk on the RIGHT to face oncoming traffic. The exception to this is on approaching a blind right-hand bend, when you should cross to the left for a clearer view.

CLOTHING AND EQUIPMENT

Boots or strong, comfortable shoes are essential (on the high moors and in winter BOOTS are the ONLY suitable footwear). A windproof jacket (preferably with a hood) will be needed. Thick, heavy sweaters are not recommended — two or three lightweight layers are warmer and more adaptable to changing conditions. Denim is not at all suitable. In cold weather a woollen hat or cap will prevent the loss of a great deal of body heat. A rucsac is necessary. A small 'daysac' with a capacity of about 20 - 25 litres would be adequate for any of these walks. The author's rucsac will always contain the following items :-

- waterproof jacket and overtrousers ● small first-aid kit ● spare laces ● large-scale O.S. map ● compass ● whistle ● plastic bottle for cold drink and/or flask for coffee or soup ● a high-calorie snack (e.g. chocolate or crisps) ● dog's drinking-water in a plastic bottle with either a 'cup-top' or a separate small bowl.

In very wet, muddy conditions gaiters are an asset, once you've managed to get them on (it helps if you're a contortionist). A walking-stick is a matter of personal preference. Some walkers wouldn't be seen dead with one, but the author finds a knobstick useful for very steep, slippery descents, fording streams, beating down nettles, discouraging aggressive animals and testing potentially boggy ground prior to sinking in up to the knees. Folding, or telescopic, metal jobs which are stuffable into a rucsac are now popular, though a bit pricey.

CHILDREN

When taking children on country walks some thought must be given to the distance and the type of terrain involved. Until you're sure of the child's capabilities, keep the distances short. Most of the walks in this book would probably be too much for a child under the age of five. As a rough rule-of-thumb, a child should be able to manage about a mile for each year of his age after his fifth birthday. Children should be warmly clothed and well shod. One cannot always afford to buy expensive boots for growing feet, but at least the child should have strong shoes or close-fitting wellingtons. On no account should young children be allowed to wander off beyond the range of vision of responsible adults, and extreme care and control must be exercised in the vicinity of crags, quarries, potholes and motor-roads.

DOGS

Though dogs are generally better-behaved than children they can nevertheless present certain difficulties which the owner should bear in mind. The two main problems are livestock and stiles – particularly ladder-stiles. Dogs should be kept under close control at all times, and MUST be on a lead in the proximity of farms and farm livestock. You will be lucky to complete any of these walks without encountering cattle and/or sheep. A lead should also be used when walking on motor-roads or on moorland during nesting-time (April-June). Some large, agile dogs are able to scramble over ladder-stiles, but small models need to be lifted over, and this can sometimes be awkward if you're walking alone. If your dog is big, fat and rheumaticky then you have problems. Best places for dogs are high, open ground and woodland; worst are motor-roads and lowland pastures. On very hot, sunny days dogs can become distressed, and may be at risk of heat-stroke. On summer walks the author has in his rucsac a small, plastic spray-bottle of water.

RAMBLERS' ASSOCIATION	020 7339 8500	
2nd Floor Camelford House, 87-90 Albert Embankment, London SE1 7TW		
YORKSHIRE DALES NATIONAL PARK (GRASSINGTON)	01756 751690	
Colvend, Hebden Road, Grassington, Skipton, N Yorks BD23 5LB		
LANCASHIRE COUNTRYSIDE SERVICES	01772 534709	
PO Box 9, Winckley House, Cross Street, PRESTON PR1 8RD		
UNITED UTILITIES CATCHMENT TEAM (BOWLAND)	01200 454400	
Stocks Board House, Catlow Road, Slaidburn, Near Clitheroe BB7 3AQ		

TOURIST INFORMATION

INGLETON Community Centre	01524	241049
CLAPHAM National Park Centre	01524	251419
HORTON IN RIBBLESDALE Penyghent Café	01729	860333
SETTLE Town Hall	01729	825192
CLITHEROE Market Place	01200	425566
PRESTON The Guildhall	01772	253731

THE WALKS

No		MILES	No		MILES
1	THORNS GILL AND LING GILL	6½	16	THE RIBBLE GORGE	6¼
2	AROUND RIBBLEHEAD	6	17	BEACON HILL	6½
3	WHERNSIDE	7¾	18	PENDLE HILL	6
4	ALUM POT	4¼	19	WEST BRADFORD FELL	7¾
5	POTHOLES OF BIRKWITH	7	20	BASHALL AND WADDINGTON	6½
6	PENYGHENT AND PLOVER HILL	8¼	21	GREAT MITTON	5¾
7	HORTON AND HELWITH BRIDGE	5½	22	WHALLEY AND OLD LANGHO	6½
8	WATERFALLS OF STAINFORTH	5½	23	LONGRIDGE FELL	7
9	GIGGLESWICK SCAR	5½	24	HURST GREEN AND DUTTON	5½
10	THE SETTLE CAVES	5	25	DINCKLEY	5½
11	SOUTH FROM SETTLE	5¼	26	RIBCHESTER	6
12	THE INGS OF RIBBLE	7¼	27	OSBALDESTON	5½
13	LONG PRESTON	6	28	LONGRIDGE AND KNOWLE GREEN	5½
14	HELLIFIELD	6¼	29	LONGTON MARSHES	5
15	PAYTHORNE AND GISBURNE PARK	5½	30	THE RIBBLE ESTUARY	7

LOCATION OF WALKS
AND
MAPS REQUIRED

ORDNANCE SURVEY MAPS NEEDED TO COVER THE AREA

A **OUTDOOR LEISURE 2 YORKSHIRE DALES** Southern and Western areas.

B **OUTDOOR LEISURE 41 FOREST OF BOWLAND** and Ribblesdale.

C **PATHFINDER 669** (SD 64/74) Clitheroe and Chipping.

D **PATHFINDER 680** (SD 63/73) Longridge and Great Harwood.

E **PATHFINDER 688** (SD 42/52) Preston (South) and Leyland.

F **PATHFINDER 678** (SD 32/33) Blackpool.

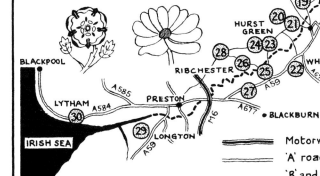

Motorway

'A' roads

'B' and minor roads

R. Ribble

WALK	STARTING POINT	MAP REQUIRED
1	RIBBLEHEAD	A
2	RIBBLEHEAD	A
3	RIBBLEHEAD	A
4	SELSIDE	A
5	HORTON IN RIBBLESDALE	A
6	HORTON IN RIBBLESDALE	A
7	HORTON IN RIBBLESDALE	A
8	STAINFORTH	A OR B
9	GIGGLESWICK	B
10	SETTLE	A OR B
11	SETTLE	A OR B
12	RATHMELL	B
13	LONG PRESTON	A OR B
14	HELLIFIELD	B
15	PAYTHORNE	B
16	GISBURN	B
17	SAWLEY	B OR C
18	DOWNHAM	B
19	WEST BRADFORD	B OR C
20	EDISFORD BRIDGE (CLITHEROE)	B OR C
21	EDISFORD BRIDGE (CLITHEROE)	B
22	WHALLEY	D
23	HURST GREEN	C AND D
24	HURST GREEN	D
25	MARLES WOOD	D
26	RIBCHESTER	D
27	OSBALDESTON	D
28	LONGRIDGE	D
29	LONGTON	E
30	LYTHAM	E AND F

ABOUT THIS BOOK

THE WALKS

All the walks described in this book are circular, and begin at a place where a car may be parked without causing an obstruction. They are fairly uniform in length, an average of 6¼ miles making them half-day rather than full-day excursions. The routes, which adhere to public rights-of-way and permissive paths, should be free from serious difficulty and well within the capability of reasonably fit and agile walkers. Although the author has personally researched and walked all these routes, it must be pointed out that changes will occur quite frequently. Walkers may expect to encounter new stiles and fences and possibly diversions – either temporary or permanent. In such cases please note and obey legitimate waymarks and signs.

Neither the author nor the publisher can accept responsibility for any accident or misadventure incurred on these walks.

THE MAPS

The strip-maps show all relevant route-finding features, and great care has been taken to ensure accuracy, although for the sake of clarity there is deliberate distortion of scale in depicting routes along, for example, narrow lanes or through farmyards. In all maps north is at the top. In the Route Directions any mention of a stile, gate or footbridge means that it is used, unless otherwise stated. The maps and route directions together should suffice to make it quite clear to you how you've got lost. It is, however, strongly recommended that an Ordnance Survey map be carried, as this will add interest and enable the walker to identify distant features not mentioned in the text. A full list of the Ordnance Survey maps required to cover the area can be found on Page 9.

SYMBOLS USED ON THE MAPS

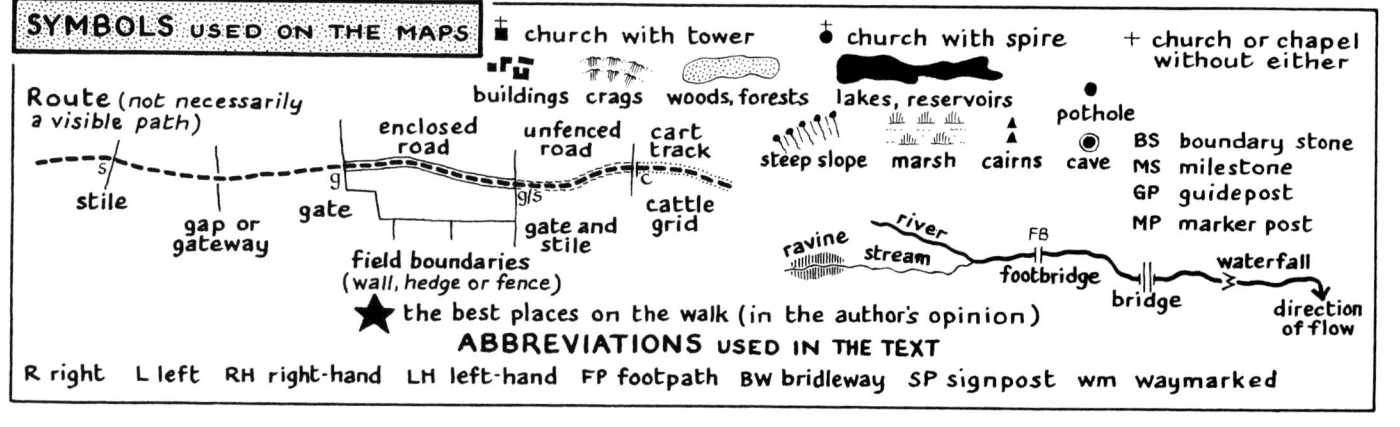

church with tower   church with spire   + church or chapel without either

Route (not necessarily a visible path)

stile   gap or gateway   gate   enclosed road   unfenced road   cart track   cattle grid   gate and stile   field boundaries (wall, hedge or fence)

buildings   crags   woods, forests   lakes, reservoirs   pothole

steep slope   marsh   cairns   cave

BS boundary stone
MS milestone
GP guidepost
MP marker post

ravine   river   stream   footbridge   bridge   waterfall   direction of flow

★ the best places on the walk (in the author's opinion)

ABBREVIATIONS USED IN THE TEXT

R right   L left   RH right-hand   LH left-hand   FP footpath   BW bridleway   SP signpost   wm waymarked

THE SOURCE OF THE RIBBLE

The Ribble, like most other rivers, has no obvious and indisputable source, for its headwaters issue from a multitude of widely-scattered moorland springs. The Ordnance Survey uses the name 'Ribblehead' for a vague area around the junction (765 792) of the roads B6255 and B6479 where the river – hereabouts known as Thorns Gill – is already well-established. Exactly where Thorns Gill becomes the River Ribble is not clear, so perhaps from the point of view of nomenclature the 'Ribble' should be regarded as starting near Selside with the arrival of the waters of Cam Beck (791 763). The Patron Saint of North Country walkers, Alfred Wainwright, in his 'Ribble Sketchbook', suggests the source as being the roadside confluence of Ouster Gill and Long Gill (793 819), but this would seem purely arbitrary with no geographical justification. Ouster Gill has its origins in a couple of springs at about 1600' on the south-east slopes of Wold Fell (792 844). However, Long Gill and its tributary Jam Sike can be followed by a right-of-way footpath up to a spring on Gayle Moor (813 831) at an altitude of about 1870', which would therefore seem to have the strongest claim to be regarded as the true source.

HEADWATERS OF THE RIBBLE

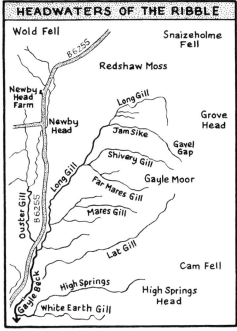

Wold Fell
B6255
Snaizeholme Fell
Redshaw Moss
Newby Head Farm
Newby Head
Long Gill
Grove Head
Jam Sike
Gavel Gap
Shivery Gill
Gayle Moor
Far Mares Gill
Mares Gill
Ouster Gill
B6255
Lat Gill
Cam Fell
Long Gill
High Springs
High Springs Head
Gayle Beck
White Earth Gill

HOW TO GET THERE

Hawes
The prominent hill is Snaizeholme Fell
Newby Head Farm
B6255
Dent
RW sign
resurgence
fold
butt
broken wall
Ingleton
hut
bracken
wall
Long Gill
Long Gill
Jam Sike
Gavel Gap
blocked gateway
Shivery Gill
springs
wall
Far Mares Gill

3 MILES THERE AND BACK

Follow a path heading directly away from the road, and in about 100yds turn R along a faint path. It soon gets clearer, and briefly becomes a broad, rough track as it passes a ruined sheepfold known as 'The Round'. The path swings L to reach an ugly little concrete hut, then L again to head up the valley as a thin trod. Where the stream forks cross it to a cairn and a clear path climbing to the L of the tiny gill. Ignore a right fork crossing the stream. Bear R to climb alongside crosswall until you reach a wall junction. A few yds to the R is a tiny spring at the base of an outcrop.

WHEN TO GET THERE: IDEALLY ON A COLD, CLEAR, FROSTY WINTER'S DAY.
SOGGY IN WET WEATHER AND UNPLEASANT IN MIST.

P Newby Head. Drive to the junction of the B6255 Ingleton-Hawes road and the Newby Head - Dent road. There is roadside parking space.
Map ref: 805 835

ROUTE DIRECTIONS

The official right-of-way starts about 100yds N of the road junction (FP Gavel Gap 1⅝ and RW sign). However, there is no path initially across the rough moor, and it is simpler to start from the little bridge opposite the junction.

1 THORNS GILL & LING GILL — 6½ MILES

P Ribblehead. Park near Gearstones Lodge, on the B6255 Ingleton - Hawes road 1 mile E of its junction with the B6479 Horton road. Ample roadside parking space just to W of buildings. Map ref: 778 799

Map labels

Dent Head 2¼, Hawes, Gayle Beck, ROMAN ROAD, Dales Way, Pennine Way, 6P x, Dales Way, Pennine Way, Cam End 1437', Long Bank, barn, barn, B6255, Ingleton, Gearstones Lodge, Holme Hill Cave (10), Round Hill, Thorns Gill, Capnut Cave (no access at present), Cove Hole, Thorns, Pennine Way, barn, Thorns Moss, wall, Crutchin Gill, boggy, broad stony track, Cam Beck, Ling Gill Bridge (8), Ling Gill, Ling Gill Pot, North Fair Bottom Cave, Coppice Cave, Fair Bottom Hill, ford, wet ground, ford, s fence, Low Rigg, Swinesett Hill, clump of trees, wall, Nether Lodge (5), God's Bridge, kiln, Dry Lathe (barn), Cave Hill, Browgill Cave, Cam Beck, Five Minute Hole, Calf Holes, A, B, wall, Pennine Way, Old Ing, plantation

NOTE: A visit to BROWGILL CAVE requires a short (250yd) detour. To approach from _below_, turn L after crossing stream at God's Bridge and climb with wall on L. From _above_, cross ladder-stile on L just beyond Calf Holes and descend with wall on R. These are not rights-of-way, but are much-used by potholers.

Take a peep inside this barn to see the old-fashioned cattle-stalls

THORNS (now ruinous) and **NETHER LODGE** (a focal point of several footpaths) were both formerly granges of Furness Abbey.

ROUTE DIRECTIONS

① Take gate/ladder-stile (BW Ford only. FP Thorns) at parking-place and descend with wall on L. Cross footbridge and climb, with wall on R, over hill and down to barns at Thorns. ② Go R over ladder-stile into walled track. At small barn go through gate (FP Nether Lodge 1¼), forward to ladder-stile and follow wall on L over hill and down to barn. ③ Go round far side of barn to cross wall-stile. Green path leads away, in a few yards swinging R (towards Penyghent). Cross ladder-stile and bear slightly R over hill to pick up fairly clear path. Ford two streams (only tidgy ones) then climb to stile (with duckboards) in fence on skyline. ④ Ignore path bearing R. Head for farm on sketchy path. ⑤ Take ladder-stile (SP Birkwith) to pass to R of house. Follow track by wall, cross bridge and turn L (FP High Birkwith) to ladder-stile and cart-track beyond (FP High Birkwith). Cross another ladder-stile (where stream runs under track), then forward alongside wall on R to eventually join another cart-track. ⑥ At T-junction, just beyond a plantation, turn L up farm road. ⑦ Through gate and turn L (SP Pennine Way) along cart-track. ⑧ Cross bridge and turn R to climb stony moorland track. ⑨ At T-junction (with guidepost) turn L down Dales Way. ⑩ Cross big footbridge and forward to cross ladder-stile. Detour L for 100 yards to view Holme Hill Cave, then return to track and follow it up to road. Turn L along road back to Gearstones.

Moderately strenuous. Varied terrain with many interesting features. First 1¾ miles, to Nether Lodge, can be damp underfoot. From Nether Lodge the walk is entirely on good, firm tracks. Between points ⑧ and ⑩ the route is very exposed, and consequently the walk cannot be recommended in bad weather. ½ mile on a motor-road (with open grass verges). 11 ladder-stiles (all but one with adjacent gates).

GEARSTONES

GEARSTONES was formerly an inn on the old Lancaster to Richmond coach road. There are many local tales of uproarious goings-on at Gearstones in the 1870s, when the railway and viaduct were being built and thousands of thirsty navvies lived just up the road in a shanty town called Batty Green. It ceased to function as an inn in 1911.

TWO FINE RESURGENCE CAVES

Browgill Cave

Holme Hill Cave

LING GILL

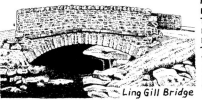
Ling Gill Bridge

THIS WOODED LIMESTONE GORGE IS ONE OF THE MOST DRAMATIC RAVINES IN THE YORKSHIRE DALES. HERE CAM BECK SWIRLS AND CASCADES THROUGH A CHAOTIC JUMBLE OF HUGE BOULDERS, WHILST ABOVE THIS MAELSTROM NEAR-VERTICAL WALLS OF ROCK RISE TO SOME 200'. IT IS A NATIONAL NATURE RESERVE, BUT IS NOT OPEN TO THE PUBLIC DUE TO ITS DANGEROUS SLOPES. WITHIN THE GORGE IS PRESERVED MUCH OF THE NATURAL VEGETATION OF THE LIMESTONE FELLS. THE STURDY OLD GRITSTONE PACKHORSE BRIDGE HAS AN INSCRIBED TABLET (NOW SCARCELY DECIPHERABLE) INFORMING US THAT THE BRIDGE WAS REPAIRED IN 1765 'AT THE CHARGE OF THE WHOLE WEST RIDEING'.

THE CAVES AND POTHOLES

With the exception of Browgill Cave (see notes on previous page), all the caves and potholes mentioned are close to the route and easily located. To find **COVE HOLE** go a few yards past the ladder-stile at point ②, to where a small stream goes underground. **FIVE MINUTE HOLE** has a tiny entrance beneath a limestone outcrop to the R of the track. Not very exciting. **GOD'S BRIDGE** is a 60' long 'through' cave where Brow Gill flows under the track. Don't be tempted to walk through it — it's full of deep pools. **BROWGILL CAVE** is one of the finest in the district and, when the water-level is very low, may be safely explored for about 70 yards. Above the cave is a splendid limekiln. **CALF HOLES**, popular with cavers, is an impressive rocky stream sink. Don't get too near the edge - slippery rock. The stream is that which emerges at Browgill. **COPPICE CAVE** and **NORTH FAIR BOTTOM CAVE** are located 30 yards to the R of the track just before reaching a clump of six trees. The former is a shaft in a small shakehole; the latter is a small stream sink. **LING GILL POT** is a small slot in a dry streambed 20 yards to R of track just beyond a notice board. The sound of an underground waterfall can be heard. **HOLME HILL CAVE**, a resurgence about 100 yards to L of track, has a fine stream passage but the water is usually too deep to enter.

ROUTE DIRECTIONS

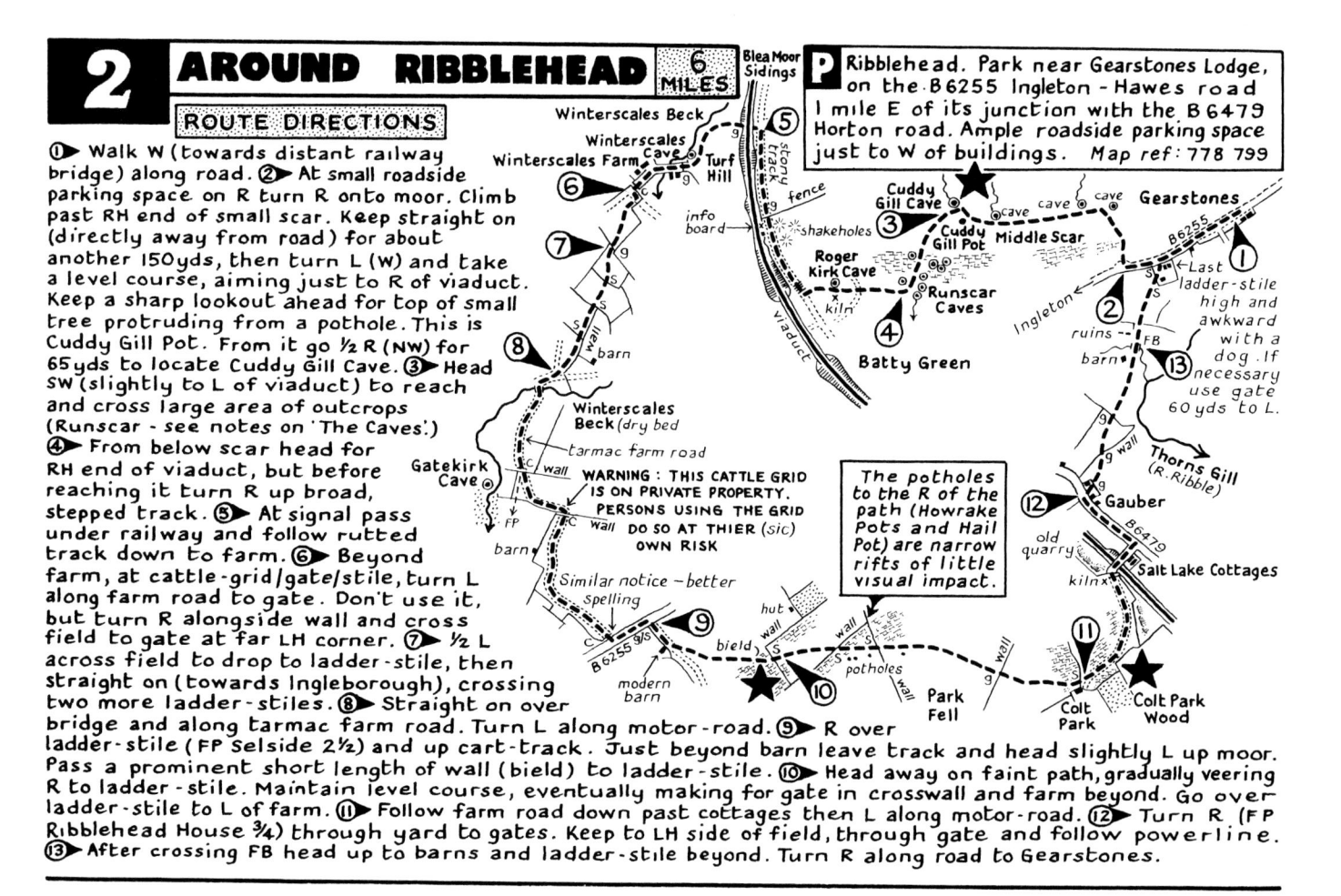

P Ribblehead. Park near Gearstones Lodge, on the B6255 Ingleton - Hawes road 1 mile E of its junction with the B6479 Horton road. Ample roadside parking space just to W of buildings. Map ref: 778 799

①▶ Walk W (towards distant railway bridge) along road. **②▶** At small roadside parking space on R turn R onto moor. Climb past RH end of small scar. Keep straight on (directly away from road) for about another 150yds, then turn L (W) and take a level course, aiming just to R of viaduct. Keep a sharp lookout ahead for top of small tree protruding from a pothole. This is Cuddy Gill Pot. From it go ½ R (NW) for 65yds to locate Cuddy Gill Cave. **③▶** Head SW (slightly to L of viaduct) to reach and cross large area of outcrops (Runscar - see notes on 'The Caves'.) **④▶** From below scar head for RH end of viaduct, but before reaching it turn R up broad, stepped track. **⑤▶** At signal pass under railway and follow rutted track down to farm. **⑥▶** Beyond farm, at cattle-grid/gate/stile, turn L along farm road to gate. Don't use it, but turn R alongside wall and cross field to gate at far LH corner. **⑦▶** ½ L across field to drop to ladder-stile, then straight on (towards Ingleborough), crossing two more ladder-stiles. **⑧▶** Straight on over bridge and along tarmac farm road. Turn L along motor-road. **⑨▶** R over ladder-stile (FP Selside 2½) and up cart-track. Just beyond barn leave track and head slightly L up moor. Pass a prominent short length of wall (bield) to ladder-stile. **⑩▶** Head away on faint path, gradually veering R to ladder-stile. Maintain level course, eventually making for gate in crosswall and farm beyond. Go over ladder-stile to L of farm. **⑪▶** Follow farm road down past cottages then L along motor-road. **⑫▶** Turn R (FP Ribblehead House ¾) through yard to gates. Keep to LH side of field, through gate and follow powerline. **⑬▶** After crossing FB head up to barns and ladder-stile beyond. Turn R along road to Gearstones.

WARNING: THIS CATTLE GRID IS ON PRIVATE PROPERTY. PERSONS USING THE GRID DO SO AT THIER (sic) OWN RISK

Similar notice — better spelling

The potholes to the R of the path (Howrake Pots and Hail Pot) are narrow rifts of little visual impact.

Last ladder-stile high and awkward with a dog. If necessary use gate 60 yds to L.

Map labels: Blea Moor Sidings, Winterscales Beck, Winterscales Cave, Winterscales Farm, Turf Hill, info board, shakeholes, Cuddy Gill Cave, Cuddy Gill Pot, Middle Scar, Gearstones, cave, cave, Roger Kirk Cave, Runscar Caves, kiln, Batty Green, fence, stony track, Ingleton, ruins, barn, Thorns Gill (R. Ribble), Gauber, old quarry, Salt Lake Cottages, kiln, Winterscales Beck (dry bed, tarmac farm road, barn, Gatekirk Cave, FP, barn, B6255 S/S, modern barn, hut, wall, bield, potholes, Park Fell, Colt Park, Colt Park Wood, viaduct

Easy walking with very little uphill work. 9 ladder-stiles (2 with adjacent gates). ¾ mile on motor-roads. Ribblehead is bleak and dismal in appearance, but has many hidden charms (a bit like the author, really). The cave-hunting is jolly good fun, the views of the celebrated 'Three Peaks' are superb – Ingleborough in particular looks quite awesome – and the famous Ribblehead Viaduct* may be admired from every conceivable angle.

* Its proper name is 'Batty Moss Viaduct', but nobody calls it that.

THE CAVES

Runscar Cave

Roger Kirk Cave

The area is riddled with caves and potholes. Only those easily located and readily identified are shown, but you will probably stumble upon (hopefully not into) others as you wander across Runscar Common. CUDDY GILL POT is an impressive surface crater 30ft deep and easily descended at its E end. CUDDY GILL CAVE'S main entrance is where a small stream sinks, but there is easier access 10 yds away through a natural rock archway. The cave can normally be safely explored, but after heavy rain may flood to the roof. Dotted around Runscar are 7 cave entrances known as THISTLE CAVES and RUNSCAR CAVES. The most imposing entrance (illustrated) is in a depression just below the scar. An underground stream is visible. The main entrance (illustrated) to ROGER KIRK CAVE lies just to the N of an old kiln. It faces the viaduct, and a small stream emerges. WINTERSCALES CAVE is in a limestone scar on the S bank of the beck 200 yds upstream of the bridge. The small entrance is not too easy to find. There is no public access to GATEKIRK CAVE, which is a pity, for this is a fine cave of debouchure at the head of a lovely wooded gill.

COLT PARK WOOD

is a fragment of ancient ash woodland clothing a limestone pavement. The rich variety of flora includes such flowers as bird's-eye primrose, herb robert, mountain pansy, globe flower (illustrated) and the rare baneberry. The wood is a nature reserve and may not be visited without a permit.

This short, curved wall at point ⑩ serves as an animal shelter, or bield. It is solidly constructed, and has a look of great antiquity.

BATTY GREEN
1875-1991

DURING RAILWAY BUILDING SOME 3,000 MEN AND THEIR FAMILIES LIVED HERE IN A TEMPORARY NAVVY TOWNSHIP, OR SHANTY TOWN. THE PLACE WAS A HIVE OF ACTIVITY, WITH SAWMILLS, BLACKSMITHS' FORGES, A NETWORK OF TRAMWAYS AND RAILWAYS, AND KILNS PRODUCING 20,000 BRICKS A DAY TO LINE THE VIADUCT'S ARCHES. THE TOWNSHIP HAD A WIDE RANGE OF FACILITIES, INCLUDING A SCHOOL, HOSPITAL, CHAPEL, LIBRARY, POST OFFICE AND SHOPS, BUT LIVING CONDITIONS WERE SQUALID, THE WINTERS WERE HARSH AND LIFE WAS TOUGH. OUTBREAKS OF SMALLPOX CLAIMED SO MANY VICTIMS THAT AN UNMARKED MASS GRAVE HAD TO BE DUG IN THE CHURCHYARD OF ST. LEONARD'S AT NEARBY CHAPEL-LE-DALE.

Detail from the memorial plaque, Ribblehead viaduct.

THERE WERE SEVERAL OTHER SHANTY TOWNS IN THE AREA, AND THEIR NAMES ARE SHOWN ON THE MEMORIAL PLAQUE BELOW THE VIADUCT. ONE WAS SALT LAKE, WHERE NOW STANDS A ROW OF RAILWAY COTTAGES. NOTE THE FINE LIMEKILN AND THE BIG QUARRY WHICH YIELDED MUCH OF THE STONE FOR THE VIADUCT.

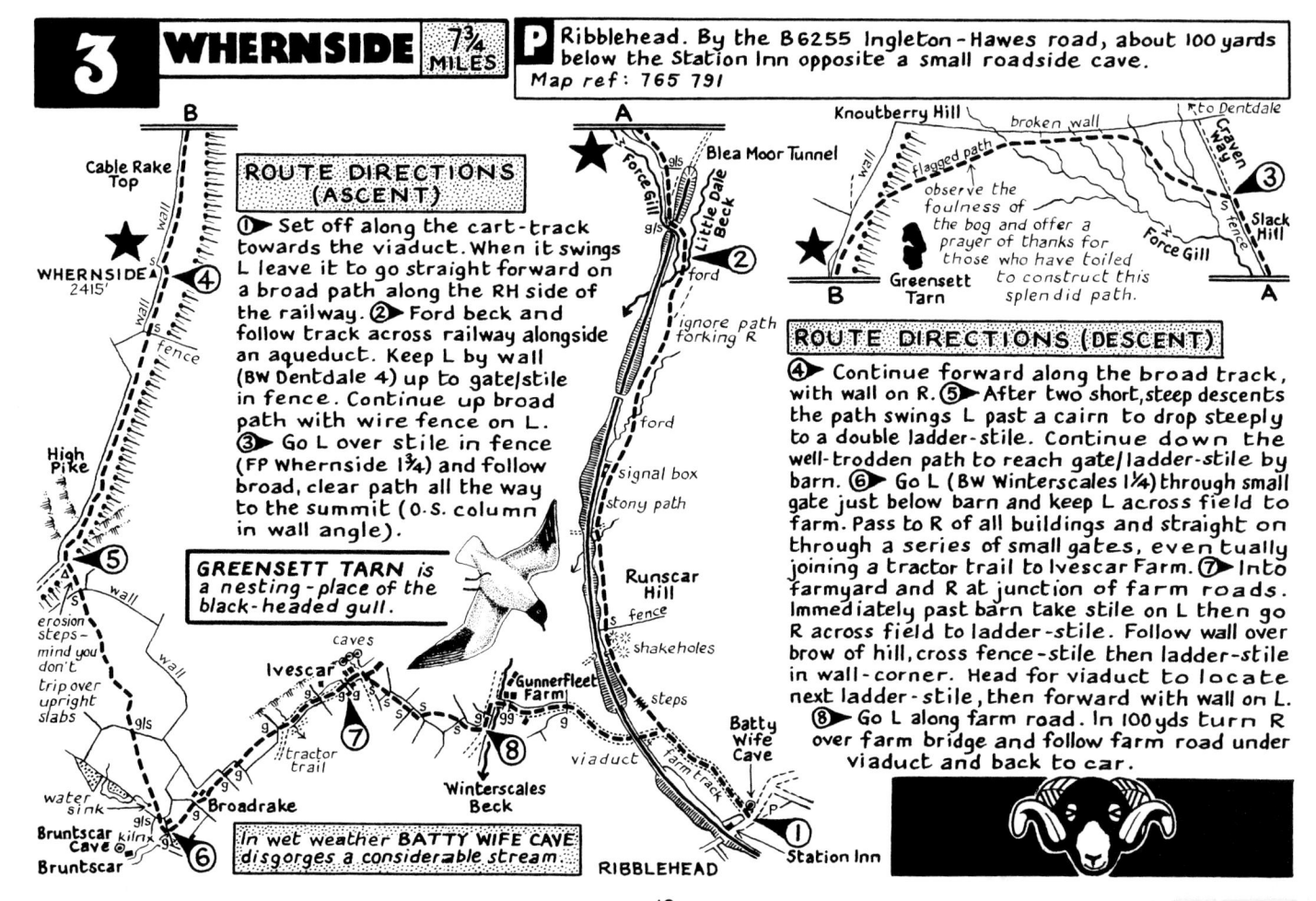

3 WHERNSIDE 7¾ MILES

P Ribblehead. By the B6255 Ingleton-Hawes road, about 100 yards below the Station Inn opposite a small roadside cave.
Map ref: 765 791

ROUTE DIRECTIONS (ASCENT)

① Set off along the cart-track towards the viaduct. When it swings L leave it to go straight forward on a broad path along the RH side of the railway. ② Ford beck and follow track across railway alongside an aqueduct. Keep L by wall (BW Dentdale 4) up to gate/stile in fence. Continue up broad path with wire fence on L. ③ Go L over stile in fence (FP Whernside 1¾) and follow broad, clear path all the way to the summit (O.S. column in wall angle).

GREENSETT TARN is a nesting-place of the black-headed gull.

In wet weather BATTY WIFE CAVE disgorges a considerable stream.

observe the foulness of the bog and offer a prayer of thanks for those who have toiled to construct this splendid path.

ROUTE DIRECTIONS (DESCENT)

④ Continue forward along the broad track, with wall on R. ⑤ After two short, steep descents the path swings L past a cairn to drop steeply to a double ladder-stile. Continue down the well-trodden path to reach gate/ladder-stile by barn. ⑥ Go L (BW Winterscales 1¼) through small gate just below barn and keep L across field to farm. Pass to R of all buildings and straight on through a series of small gates, eventually joining a tractor trail to Ivescar Farm. ⑦ Into farmyard and R at junction of farm roads. Immediately past barn take stile on L then go R across field to ladder-stile. Follow wall over brow of hill, cross fence-stile then ladder-stile in wall-corner. Head for viaduct to locate next ladder-stile, then forward with wall on L. ⑧ Go L along farm road. In 100 yds turn R over farm bridge and follow farm road under viaduct and back to car.

Map labels

B — Cable Rake Top — WHERNSIDE 2415' — High Pike — erosion steps – mind you don't trip over upright slabs — water sink — Bruntscar Cave — Bruntscar — Broadrake — tractor trail — Ivescar — caves — Winterscales Beck — Gunnerfleet Farm — viaduct — farm track — Batty Wife Cave — Station Inn — RIBBLEHEAD — P

A — Force Gill — Blea Moor Tunnel — Little Dale Beck — ford — ignore path forking R — ford — signal box — stony path — Runscar Hill — fence — shakeholes — steps

Knoutberry Hill — broken wall — to Dentdale — Craven Way — flagged path — wall — Slack Hill — Force Gill — Greensett Tarn — B — A

16

3

Strenuous, with a 2¼-mile-long climb of 1,300' from the aqueduct to the summit. Should not be attempted in severe wintry conditions. The walk is almost entirely on good tracks and paths, and is perfectly safe – though perhaps a waste of energy – in mist. After heavy or prolonged rain the fording of Little Dale Beck may prove difficult (tip - pop a couple of plastic bin-liners into your rucksack). The views are quite breathtaking. 6 ladder-stiles (2 with adjacent gates). No motor-roads.

THE SETTLE-CARLISLE RAILWAY
A MARVEL OF VICTORIAN ENGINEERING

The story of the building of this famous railway is one of enthusiasm, determination and, above all, incredible toil and hardship during some of the worst winters of the 19th C. The ambitious project was begun in November 1869, when the first sod was cut near Settle Junction. After the construction of 72 miles of track, 325 bridges, 21 viaducts, 14 tunnels and 103 culverts, the line was declared open on 2 August 1875. The best-known and most stunning feature of the whole colossal enterprise is the mighty, 24-arch RIBBLEHEAD VIADUCT (properly called Batty Moss Viaduct), the first stone of which was laid on 12 October 1870. The foundations had to be sunk 25' through peat and clay to solid rock, and there were countless other problems – the hardness of the stone, flooding of the quarries, the sogginess of the moor, blizzards, and winds so violent that the brickies were unable to work for fear of being blown off the scaffolding. The quarter-mile-long, 104' high viaduct was completed in October 1874. Following recent restoration work a most interesting commemorative stone was placed below the 14th arch. Some 300 miners, bricklayers and labourers were employed in building BLEA MOOR TUNNEL. Progressing at the rate of about 16 yards a week they took 5 years to finish the job. The tunnel is 2629 yards long and at one point is 500' below the surface of the moor. One of the 3 ventilation shafts is 360' deep. The thousands of navvies engaged on this work lived in 'shanty towns', the names of which can be found on the aforementioned commemorative stone.

FOR NOTES ON BATTY GREEN SHANTY TOWN SEE WALK 2

The broad path climbing Slack Hill is none-too-inspiring, but the monotony is relieved by the splendid beck scenery down on the left. FORCE GILL has two fine waterfalls; the lower one is well-seen from the path, but only the top little bit of the upper one (called 'The Mare's Tail') is visible.

The path crosses a series of small culverts near the broken wall on Knoutberry Hill.

WHERNSIDE

Although the highest of the famous 'Three Peaks' and, indeed, the highest Dales summit, Whernside is not blessed with such dramatic profiles as are Ingleborough and Penyghent. In fact it has to be conceded that from most angles it looks pretty boring. The summit, too, is dreary, but the walk to it, and from it, along the rim of the plunging escarpment, is sheer bliss. The retrospective view is of the Howgills and the exquisite Dentdale beyond the extensive Whernside Tarns. Away to the left the Dales fells stretch seemingly to infinity, whilst ahead looms the majestic Ingleborough. A steep descent takes us down to some attractive limestone pastures and gentle meadow paths.

The summit

4 ALUM POT — 4¼ MILES

ALUM POT IS ON PRIVATE LAND, AND A SMALL ACCESS FEE IS PAYABLE AT SELSIDE FARM. PAY AS YOU PASS THROUGH SELSIDE AT THE END OF THE WALK. (TO PAY AT THE START, AND THEN HAPPEN TO FALL DOWN THE POTHOLE, WOULD BE AN UNFORTUNATE WASTE OF MONEY).

P At Selside, on the B6479 between Ribblehead and Horton in Ribblesdale. Parking space in the rough lane just to the north of the hamlet, opposite Top Farm. Map ref: 783 756

① Walk up rough lane to go straight ahead through gate/stile and up stony track to the walled and wooded Alum Pot. ② At far side of pot cross stream and follow clear path up to the fenced Diccan Pot (near the wall). Turn L and follow wall to Lower and Upper Long Churn Caves (also fenced). Continue by wall, cross ladder-stile and clints to locate Upper Long Churn Cave entrance (position marked by tree). ③ Retrace steps to gate/stile at top of rough lane and turn R along green track between walls to gate/stile. ④ Go forward with wall on R. At wall-corner bear L to ladder-stile near gate and trough. ⑤ Maintain direction, keeping about 50 yards from wall on L. Through gate/ladder-stile and follow wall on L, turning L with it down cart-track. ⑥ At junction with farm road turn 90° R (no path) and cross field to re-join farm road. ⑦ Straight through farmyard then fork L (wm) through gate. A few yards below gate go R over step-stile then L to ladder-stile. ⑧ Cross broken wall and aim for LH end of Penyghent to descend to gate/ladder-stile. ⑨ Walk R along road. ⑩ Cross ladder-stile (FP Selside) on L and go L across rough field to ladder-stile in crosswall. ⑪ Maintain direction and height (the tendency here is to drop too far to the R) across another rough field to gate/ladder-stile in crosswall. Straight on parallel with wall on R (intermittent path) to ladder-stile. Keep straight ahead to reach gate onto road at second group of cottages. ⑫ Turn R to follow road through Selside. Turn R at the small village green to locate Selside Farm, and there pay your fee (30p at the time of writing, and worth every penny).

☠☠ **DANGER!** The wall encircling Alum Pot is provided with ladder-stiles to facilitate access by potholers. If you feel you *must* cross the wall, then you do so at your peril. **ONE FALSE MOVE COULD BE FATAL.**

SIMPLIFIED PLAN OF THE LONG CHURN – ALUM POT CAVE SYSTEM

- ≈≈≈ stream passage
- — surface stream
- ≈ dry passage
- ---- route of walk

Lower Long Churn Cave
Upper Long Churn Cave (exit)
resurgence
Diccan Pot
waterfall
passages at different levels
Lower Long Churn Cave
resurgence
Upper Long Churn Cave (entrance)
clints
wall
Dr. Bannister's Hand Basin
★ good spot for a picnic
Alum Pot
Alum Pot Beck
perched boulder
→ Selside

Map labels:
Selside Farm (Pay up)
Lower Long Churn Cave
Diccan Pot
Upper Long Churn Cave (exit)
Upper Long Churn Cave (entrance)
Alum Pot
Alum Pot Beck
trough
Gill Garth
Borrins
South House
SELSIDE
North Cote Farm
Selside Cottages
Settle-Carlisle Railway
B6479
Footnaw's Hole
Turn Dub
The Tarn
R. Ribble
Low Moor
→ Horton
wall / broken wall

A short, easy walk, the highlight of which is a visit to an awesome pothole and a fascinating series of caves. Mostly on cart-tracks and pathless pastures, with the last ½ mile along a motor-road. 14 ladder-stiles (6 with adjacent gates). The circular section of the walk, though pleasant enough, is a bit of an anti-climax after the excitement of Alum Pot and Co. Best time to go is after heavy rain in winter (in summer the pothole is partially obscured by foliage). Take two good torches.

ALUM POT

ALUM POT, Britain's most spectacular pothole, is a stupendous surface-gash 120' long and 35' wide surrounded by windswept larches and pines planted in 1874. ALUM POT BECK flows over the southern lip of the chasm to hurtle to the gloomy depths in a sheer 200' waterfall before cascading down for a further 100' to a final pool. In favourable light conditions you may just be able to discern, some 65' down the shaft, a shadowy opening in the vertical wall which is the dry exit of LOWER LONG CHURN CAVE. Much lower down – well beyond our range of vision – a substantial torrent plunges into the pool from the exit of DICCAN POT. The sump water drains away through impenetrable passages to re-appear at FOOTNAW'S HOLE, a disgustingly muddy 20' deep pool in a shakehole beyond Selside. From there it drains underground* once more, passing UNDER the Ribble to emerge into a pond named TURN DUB, then flowing overland to join the river as a small eastern tributary. Weird!

*In extreme flood Footnaw's Hole may overflow and drain directly into the Ribble from its west side.

Perched boulder, Alum Pot Beck

THE CAVES

DICCAN POT or DICCAN CAVE? Either name is appropriate, for this is actually a pothole (a vertical 120' pitch) within a cave. DO NOT ENTER – FOR EXPERTS ONLY. LOWER LONG CHURN CAVE (entrance) and UPPER LONG CHURN CAVE (exit) have been created by the roof collapse of a once continuous passage. 10 yards into the lower cave daylight enters through a roof 'window', and 10 yards beyond this a fine waterfall thunders in from the right. GO NO FURTHER. The low, slippery passage of the upper cave may be penetrated for about 20 yards, at which point the stream can be seen disappearing into a fissure on the left. UPPER LONG CHURN CAVE (entrance) should be left well alone, for just a few yards inside the cave the stream plunges down a 15' rock chute into a large deep pool known as Dr. Bannister's Hand Basin.

Diccan Pot

SELSIDE

SELSIDE was mentioned in the Domesday Book, but has never been more than a tiny hamlet. Until the late 19th C. an annual Pot and Cheese Fair was held here on 24th June. The barn which bears the 'Selside' nameboard is known as Selside Town Hall. Top Farm, a typical Dales longhouse, is dated 1726 but may be even older. The house called 'Shaws' has an elegant Georgian porch dated 1738, and the house opposite was once the Red Lion Inn. This would have done a roaring trade in the 1870s, when thousands of 'navvies' working on construction of the railway were living in and around Selside. Centuries ago Selside belonged to the Cistercian monks of Furness Abbey.

Selside Farm

5 POTHOLES OF BIRKWITH — 7 MILES

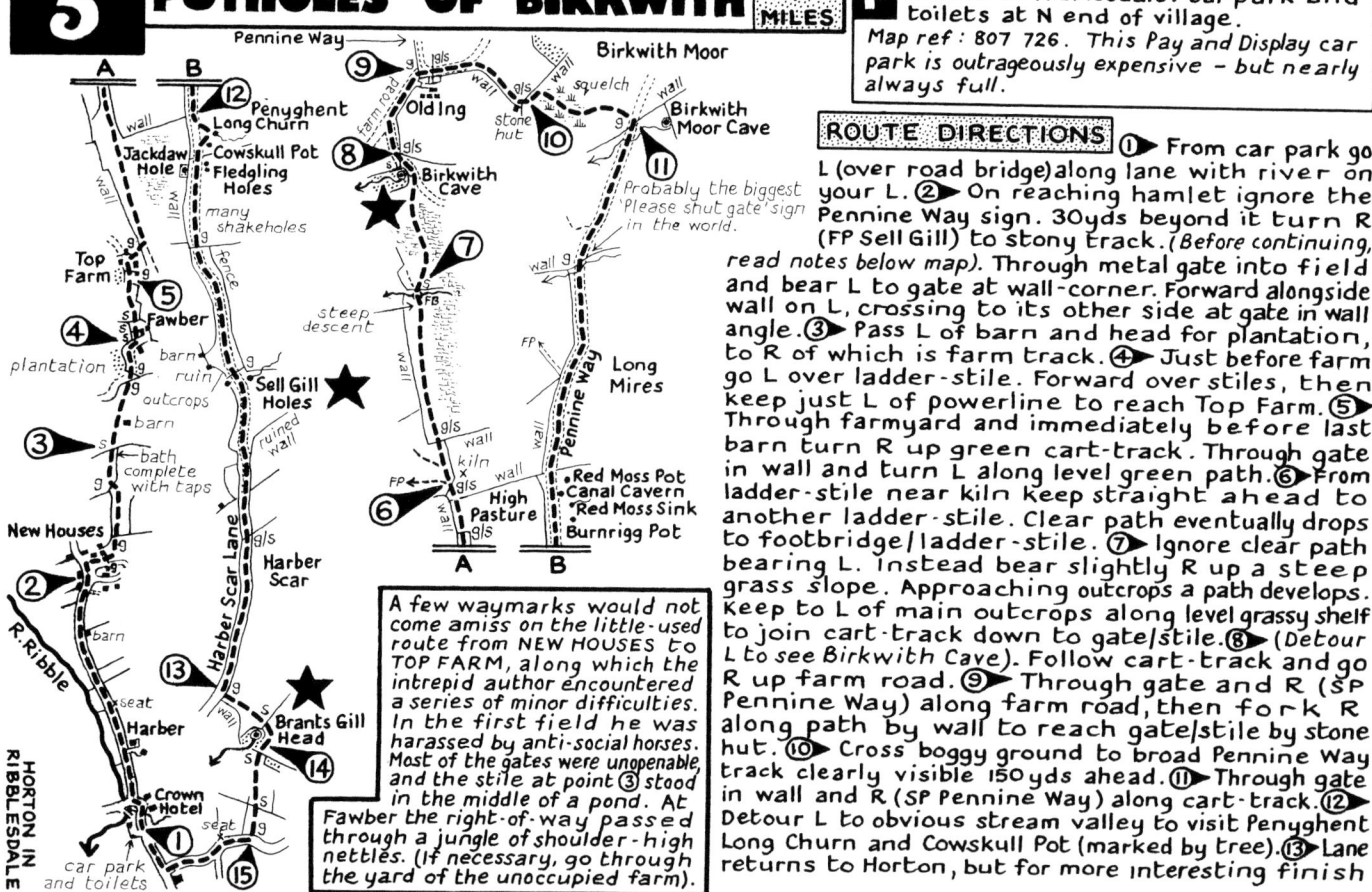

ROUTE DIRECTIONS ① From car park go L (over road bridge) along lane with river on your L. ② On reaching hamlet ignore the Pennine Way sign. 30yds beyond it turn R (FP Sell Gill) to stony track. (Before continuing, read notes below map). Through metal gate into field and bear L to gate at wall-corner. Forward alongside wall on L, crossing to its other side at gate in wall angle. ③ Pass L of barn and head for plantation, to R of which is farm track. ④ Just before farm go L over ladder-stile. Forward over stiles, then keep just L of powerline to reach Top Farm. ⑤ Through farmyard and immediately before last barn turn R up green cart-track. Through gate in wall and turn L along level green path. ⑥ From ladder-stile near kiln keep straight ahead to another ladder-stile. Clear path eventually drops to footbridge/ladder-stile. ⑦ Ignore clear path bearing L. Instead bear slightly R up a steep grass slope. Approaching outcrops a path develops. Keep to L of main outcrops along level grassy shelf to join cart-track down to gate/stile. ⑧ (Detour L to see Birkwith Cave). Follow cart-track and go R up farm road. ⑨ Through gate and R (SP Pennine Way) along farm road, then fork R along path by wall to reach gate/stile by stone hut. ⑩ Cross boggy ground to broad Pennine Way track clearly visible 150yds ahead. ⑪ Through gate in wall and R (SP Pennine Way) along cart-track. ⑫ Detour L to obvious stream valley to visit Penyghent Long Churn and Cowskull Pot (marked by tree). ⑬ Lane returns to Horton, but for more interesting finish

Map labels

Pennine Way →
Birkwith Moor
A B
⑫ Penyghent Long Churn
Jackdaw Hole
Cowskull Pot
Fledgling Holes
Top Farm
many shakeholes
⑨ gls gls wall wall squelch wall
Old Ing farm road
Stone hut
⑩
Birkwith Moor Cave
⑪
Birkwith Cave
⑧ gls
Probably the biggest 'Please shut gate' sign in the world.
④ Fawber ⑤
steep descent
barn ruin
outcrops
barn
FB
⑦
wall gls
gls
③ s bath complete with taps
ruined wall
wall kiln x gls
Long Mires
FP
Pennine Way
New Houses
② barn
Harber Scar Lane
Harber Scar
FP ←
⑥ High Pasture
gls
gls
A B
Red Moss Pot
Canal Cavern
Red Moss Sink
Burnrigg Pot
R. Ribble
⑬ seat
Harber
Brants Gill Head
⑭
Crown Hotel
seat
① car park and toilets
⑮

HORTON IN RIBBLESDALE

A few waymarks would not come amiss on the little-used route from NEW HOUSES to TOP FARM, along which the intrepid author encountered a series of minor difficulties. In the first field he was harassed by anti-social horses. Most of the gates were unopenable, and the stile at point ③ stood in the middle of a pond. At Fawber the right-of-way passed through a jungle of shoulder-high nettles. (If necessary, go through the yard of the unoccupied farm).

5

Fairly easy walking, with gentle gradients, in the heart of 'Three Peaks Country'. The walk, which abounds with interesting natural features, starts along a floriferous lane before taking us through limestone pastures to wild, rolling moorland. The return to Horton follows the Pennine Way along a splendid old packhorse road. There is a short boggy section at point ⑩. 7 ladder-stiles (5 with adjacent gates which won't necessarily open). The likelihood of encountering multitudes of sheep makes this a not-too-suitable-for-dogs walk.

take metal gate on L and climb to stile above trees. ⑭▶ Turn R and cross next wall at stile just above steep drop to stream. Bear L down field, aiming just to L of Horton church, to stile in crosswall, then down to gate. ⑮▶ R along rough lane. Keep R at fork, then R along main road.

Pen-y-ghent CAFE on the Pennine Way

i

THE CAVES AND POTHOLES

WARNING None of the caves and potholes on this walk are safe to enter. Some – Penyghent Long Churn and Sell Gill Holes for example – are palpably dangerous.

BIRKWITH CAVE: Low, wide, resurgence cave at head of wooded ravine. Impressive. **BIRKWITH MOOR CAVE:** Small entrance in rock outcrop to L of small stream. No path to it and hardly worth visiting. **RED MOSS POT:** 30 yds from track. Narrow shaft in shakehole leads to extensive cave system. **CANAL CAVERN:** Trackside rift leading to 30' pitch into stream. **RED MOSS SINK AND BURNRIGG POT:** Difficult to locate and of little visual impact. **PENYGHENT LONG CHURN:** 100 yds from track. Small stream plunges down 100' shaft. **COWSKULL POT:** In big shakehole with rowan tree. 3 entrances, one of which is 70' shaft. **FLEDGLING HOLES:** In two shakeholes near wall. Insignificant. **JACKDAW HOLE:** Huge, tree-fringed crater. **SELL GILL HOLES:** Above track is stream entrance. Below track, in small gully, is dry entrance. Both lead to massive cavern considered to be second largest in region (after Gaping Gill). **BRANTS GILL HEAD:** One of biggest resurgences in the Dales. In normal weather most of the water sinking on Penyghent re-appears here. After heavy rain excess water takes an overflow route to emerge at Douk Ghyll Scar (see Walk 7)

Sell Gill Holes – the stream entrance.

Sad and forlorn – the deserted farmhouse of Fawber

THE PENNINE WAY is a 270 mile route for masochistic walkers, its termini being Edale, in Derbyshire, and Kirk Yetholm, in Scotland's Border Country. Wayfarers who have started at Edale – the vast majority do – will limp into Horton's famous Pen-y-Ghent Cafe having completed about 92 miles of their journey.

FOR SOME NOTES ON HORTON IN RIBBLESDALE SEE WALK 7

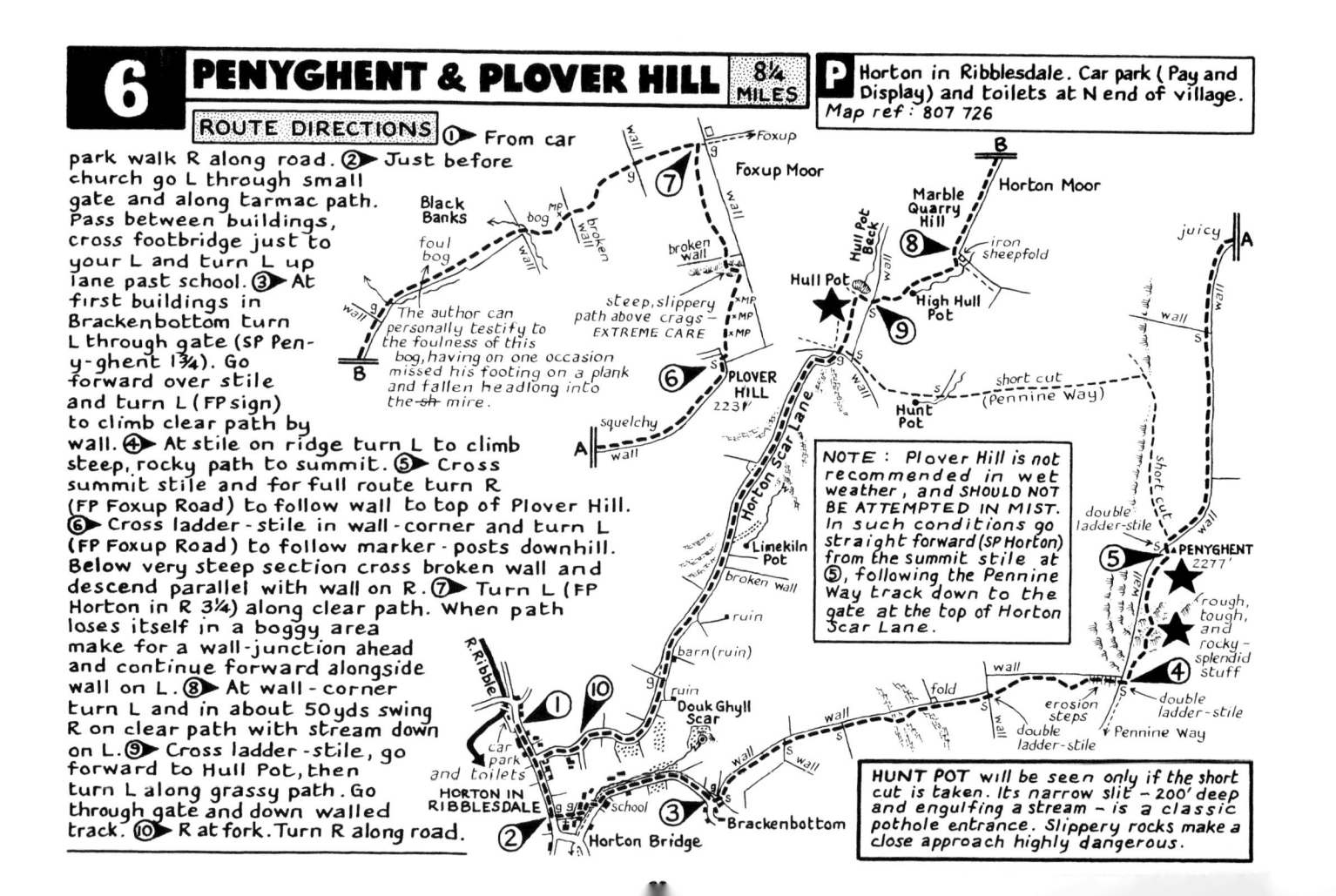

6 PENYGHENT & PLOVER HILL

8¼ MILES

P Horton in Ribblesdale. Car park (Pay and Display) and toilets at N end of village. Map ref: 807 726

ROUTE DIRECTIONS

① From car park walk R along road. ② Just before church go L through small gate and along tarmac path. Pass between buildings, cross footbridge just to your L and turn L up lane past school. ③ At first buildings in Brackenbottom turn L through gate (SP Penyghent 1¾). Go forward over stile and turn L (FP sign) to climb clear path by wall. ④ At stile on ridge turn L to climb steep, rocky path to summit. ⑤ Cross summit stile and for full route turn R (FP Foxup Road) to follow wall to top of Plover Hill. ⑥ Cross ladder-stile in wall-corner and turn L (FP Foxup Road) to follow marker-posts downhill. Below very steep section cross broken wall and descend parallel with wall on R. ⑦ Turn L (FP Horton in R 3¼) along clear path. When path loses itself in a boggy area make for a wall-junction ahead and continue forward alongside wall on L. ⑧ At wall-corner turn L and in about 50yds swing R on clear path with stream down on L. ⑨ Cross ladder-stile, go forward to Hull Pot, then turn L along grassy path. Go through gate and down walled track. ⑩ R at fork. Turn R along road.

The author can personally testify to the foulness of this bog, having on one occasion missed his footing on a plank and fallen headlong into the ~~sh~~ mire.

NOTE : Plover Hill is not recommended in wet weather, and SHOULD NOT BE ATTEMPTED IN MIST. In such conditions go straight forward (SP Horton) from the summit stile at ⑤, following the Pennine Way track down to the gate at the top of Horton Scar Lane.

HUNT POT will be seen only if the short cut is taken. Its narrow slit – 200' deep and engulfing a stream – is a classic pothole entrance. Slippery rocks make a close approach highly dangerous.

Map labels: Foxup, Foxup Moor, Black Banks, foul bog, bog, MP, broken wall, ⑦, Hull Pot Beck, Marble Quarry Hill, Horton Moor, B, juicy, A, iron sheepfold, ⑧, Hull Pot, High Hull Pot, ⑨, steep, slippery path above crags - EXTREME CARE, MP, MP, MP, ⑥, PLOVER HILL 2231', squelchy, wall, A, Hunt Pot, short cut (Pennine Way), short cut, double ladder-stile, ⑤, PENYGHENT 2277', rough, tough, and rocky - splendid stuff, ④, double ladder-stile, Pennine Way, erosion steps, double ladder-stile, fold, wall, Horton Scar Lane, Limekiln Pot, broken wall, ruin, barn(ruin), ruin, Douk Ghyll Scar, R. Ribble, ①, ⑩, car park and toilets, HORTON IN RIBBLESDALE, ②, Horton Bridge, school, ③, Brackenbottom, B

Strenuous, with a climb of 1400' – steep and rocky in places – from Brackenbottom to the summit of Penyghent. ⅓ mile on a motor-road (with footway) and ⅓ mile on a virtually traffic-free lane. Otherwise mostly on clear paths, but with some boggy sections. 6 ladder-stiles. An optional short-cut, omitting Plover Hill, avoids most of the bogs and reduces the walk to 5½ miles.

Penyghent from the first double ladder-stile

PENYGHENT

This is one of the few Dales mountains which actually *looks* like a mountain, and its magnificent 'crouching lion' profile draws pilgrims in their thousands. Indeed, such is Penyghent's popularity that in recent years extensive work has been necessary to combat the erosion caused by the incessant pounding of boots on its various footpaths. Bands of hard gritstone resting on beds of softer, and thus more weatherworn, limestone have given the mountain its distinctive stepped outline, with 90' crags fringing the summit plateau. Although it is certainly the lowest of the famous 'Three Peaks', there would seem to be some disagreement as to Penyghent's precise height; some maps claim 2277', whilst others insist that it is only 2273'. The O.S. Leisure Guide to the Yorkshire Dales (1985) gives both these heights in different chapters! (Recent metric maps show 694m, which is 2276·9') There is also disagreement about the derivation of the name. 'Pen-y-ghent' is usually taken to mean 'Hill of the Winds', but there are those who contend that 'Hill of the Border' is more likely. Whatever the origin it is certainly an inspiring name. The extensive views from the summit take in Pendle Hill, the Bowland Fells, Morecambe Bay and South Lakeland.

PLOVER HILL

WHILST PENYGHENT WALLOWS IN NATIONWIDE FAME, ITS POOR OLD NEIGHBOUR – ONLY JUST OVER A MILE DISTANT AND A MERE 46' LOWER – LIES IN RELATIVE OBSCURITY. IT HAS TO BE ADMITTED THAT PLOVER HILL HASN'T GOT A LOT GOING FOR IT. WITH NONE OF PENYGHENT'S RUGGEDNESS, IT CAN BEST BE DESCRIBED AS A NONDESCRIPT-LOOKING LUMP. FEATURELESS, BOGGY SLOPES RISE TO AN EVEN MORE FEATURELESS AND INDETERMINATE SUMMIT WHICH IS ON PRIVATE LAND BEYOND A HIGH WALL. STILL, IT'S NICE TO SAY YOU'VE BEEN THERE AND DONE IT – BUT YOU WON'T GET A T-SHIRT.

At **HIGH HULL POT** the small stream L of the track disappears into a narrow shaft and falls in a series of pitches to a depth of over 200'. **HULL POT** is an immense crater 300' long, 60' wide and 60' deep. Hull Pot Beck can be seen flowing into the E end of the hole and sinking into the bouldery floor. In very wet weather, however, the beck reaches the chasm overland and plunges over the edge in a spectacular waterfall. In really full flood the pothole has been known to fill completely, but this is an extremely rare occurance.

A few pairs of **RAVENS** inhabit the bleak country around Penyghent. This huge bird (nearly half as large again as a rook) is both scavenger and bird of prey, and will kill rats, rabbits and even small lambs. The nest is usually built on crags or rock ledges, but occasionally a tree is used. Apart from its size, the raven is instantly recognised by its voice – a very deep croak and a distinctive, pig-like grunt.

In April the limestone outcrops near the summit of Penyghent - particularly those on the western flank of the hill overlooking the 'short cut' - are bedecked with mats of **PURPLE SAXIFRAGE**. The vivid splashes of colour look exquisite on the gleaming scars.

FOR SOME NOTES ON HORTON IN RIBBLESDALE SEE WALK 7

A corner of Horton

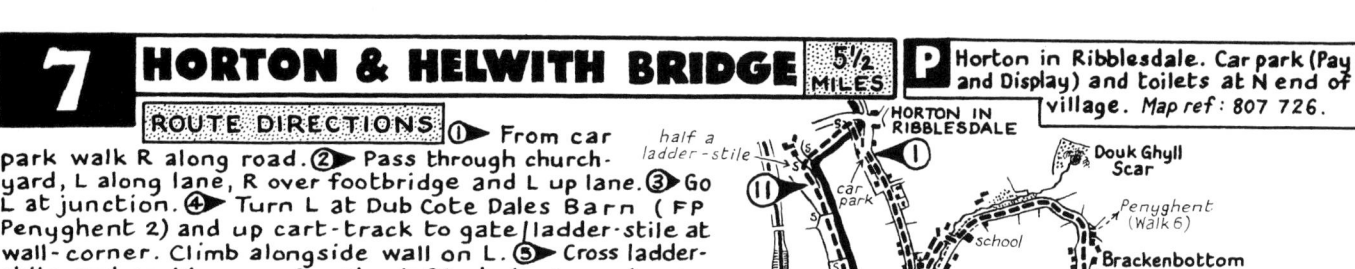

7 HORTON & HELWITH BRIDGE
5½ MILES

P Horton in Ribblesdale. Car park (Pay and Display) and toilets at N end of village. Map ref: 807 726.

ROUTE DIRECTIONS

① From car park walk R along road. ② Pass through churchyard, L along lane, R over footbridge and L up lane. ③ Go L at junction. ④ Turn L at Dub Cote Dales Barn (FP Penyghent 2) and up cart-track to gate (ladder-stile at wall-corner. Climb alongside wall on L. ⑤ Cross ladder-stile and continue up for about 60yds to a good green path slanting R up hillside. At broken wall and guidepost turn R down broad green track which soon becomes enclosed. ⑥ Go R at track-junction (FP Helwith Bridge ½ ML). ⑦ Go L down main road and R at junction to cross Helwith Bridge. ⑧ Turn R (FP Foredale ½) down steps and cross pub car park to ladder-stile. Forward over stile then bear L to stile into lane. Turn R. ⑨ Pass under railway bridge (RW sign) to follow enclosed green track to river. Ignore big footbridge – keep straight on along track. ⑩ When enclosed track ends keep straight on across field to river bank. Turn L (RW sign) to follow riverside path. It keeps close to the left bank of the river and has a few RW signs. ⑪ Approaching the houses of Horton keep L of a fence then go R through two stiles to regain river bank. At end of field climb steps to stile then R over footbridge to car park.

half a ladder-stile

HORTON IN RIBBLESDALE

car park

sewage works

school

Horton Bridge

FB

Settle

Douk Ghyll Scar

Penyghent (Walk 6)

Brackenbottom

requested route

gls wall

Dub Cote

right-of-way

Beware belligerent geese at Dub Cote

broken wall

fence

gls wall

Studfold Low Pasture

Studfold High Pasture

farm road

FB

gls

FB

ruin Cragghill Farm

private bridge (no sane person would consider crossing it anyway)

Settle Carlisle Railway

gls

boggy track

R. Ribble

FB

lane

clump of trees

fold

fold

fold

fold

Long Lane

LONG LANE has a good view of Pendle Hill, some 18 miles to the S. It's a fine track – if you're going DOWN it. Anyone you meet plodding up it will probably be bound for Penyghent

viaduct

B6479

Moor Head Lane

rest

water treatment works

HELWITH BRIDGE

Horton in Ribblesdale

A *very* easy stroll, with just one short climb of about 260' above Dub Cote. The walk follows lanes and obvious paths, and should present no route-finding problems. This is not the prettiest part of Ribblesdale, and the eye will constantly be drawn to the gigantic quarries which, though hideous to behold, have a certain grim fascination. 1¼ miles on motor-roads (mostly quiet, but at Helwith Bridge you run the risk of being flattened by huge lorries). 1½ miles of pleasant riverside walking. 6½ ladder-stiles (3 with adjacent gates). Choose a sunny autumn day to see this countryside at its colourful best.

HORTON IN RIBBLESDALE

By no means a picturesque village, but a Mecca for walkers and potholers. Horton is a long, straggling place, and has the appearance of being two separate communities set about half-a-mile apart. At the N end, near the car park, the Crown Hotel stands among a cluster of old cottages, whilst at the S end the Golden Lion faces the rugged old church. The Golden Lion was an outdoor education centre for 18 years before reverting to a pub in 1988. The church is dedicated to St. Oswald, a 7th C. King of Northumbria. It dates back at least to the reign of Henry I (1100-35) and, though much of the present building is of late 14th/early 15th C. vintage, the nave arcades, font and S. doorway have survived from the original Norman church. The W. window has panels depicting the head of Thomas à Becket and the coat-of-arms of Jervaulx Abbey. Some of the arches and walls are distinctly out of the perpendicular. Horton's old character was destroyed in late Victorian times with the building of unprepossessing houses for railway and quarry workers.

The House alongside the churchyard was originally Horton Grammar School, founded in 1725 by John Armitstead, whose table-tomb stands near the church porch.

Horton Church

● - ● ◎ ● - ●

DOUK GHYLL SCAR, A MASSIVE ROCK CIRQUE, IS PROMINENT UP ON THE LEFT FROM THE LANE TO BRACKENBOTTOM. IN THE CENTRE OF THE SCAR IS A LARGE CAVE MOUTH WHICH IN WET WEATHER DISGORGES HUGE VOLUMES OF WATER. THERE IS NO RIGHT-OF-WAY TO THE CAVE.

Double stile on riverside path

QUARRIES

Quarrying on the flanks of Moughton (pronounced 'Mooton') began towards the end of the last century, but the industry has expanded considerably since World War II. Two types of stone — limestone and slate — are quarried at Helwith Bridge where, due to the Craven Geological Fault, vertical strata of ancient Silurian rocks have been exposed beneath the horizontal layers of limestone. In bygone days thick slabs of smooth, blue-green slate were cut here to be used for such purposes as cottage floors, gateposts, gravestones and boskins (partitions in cow sheds). Nowadays it is crushed into chippings for road surfaces. Beecroft Quarry, at Horton, produces limestone.

8 WATERFALLS OF STAINFORTH — 5½ MILES

P Stainforth. Car Park (Pay and Display) and toilets by the main (B6479) Settle – Horton road. Map ref: 820 672

ROUTE DIRECTIONS

In retrospect across Ribblesdale Smearsett Scar displays a bold profile

Horton B6479

Stainforth Bridge

Tongue Gill

barn

ladder-stile in sheepfold

wall old wire fence

tractor trail

stepping stones

STAINFORTH car park, toilets

Stainforth Force

caravans

Catrigg Force

Stainforth Beck

Catrigg Beck

Cowside Beck

Upper Winskill

barn

Lower Winskill

cairn

farm road

resurgence doubles

R.Ribble

quarry

broken wall

wall

Paper Mill

seat (a good place to eat your jam butties)

barn

splendid green lane

lane

B6479

barn

seat

eyesore

Resr

LANGCLIFFE

NOTE : The usual route from Stainforth to Catrigg Force is to cross the stepping-stones and ascend a stony, enclosed track (Goat Scar Lane), but this is a weary plod. The unusual and little-used approach here described is more circuitous and more interesting. In mist, however, the Goat Scar Lane route should be preferred.

①▶ From car park walk R into village and L at T-junction. ②▶ At last house on R turn R (FP Henside Road 1¾) down enclosed track. Continue upstream. ③▶ Cross sidestream footbridge, turn L through gate into field with barn and take path slanting R up hillside. Cross broken wall at top of field, cross next field to ladder-stile and forward to follow wall on L to ladder-stile in small fold. ④▶ Follow wall on L. At wall-corner bear R over brow of hill then drop to ladder-stile at RH corner of field. Forward to cross another ladder-stile. ⑤▶ Turn R to cross nearby ladder-stile and bear slightly L across field (aim for trees on distant skyline). Cross ladder-stile and follow wall on L to cross it at ladder-stile. Descend long field to ladder-stile in RH corner. ⑥▶ Follow wall forward, crossing to its other side at gate/ladder-stile, and forward to enter walled track. Leave it immediately by a ladder-stile (SP Catrigg Foss only). Descend into hollow, where stile on L admits to path (often slippery) down to foot of waterfall. ⑦▶ Return to re-cross stiles at top of walled track and go R up gravel track to gate/ladder-stile. Turn R (SP Winskill ½) to soon re-join gravel track. ⑧▶ Cross farm road to gate/stile (FP Stainforth) and along walled track. ⑨▶ Go L over stile (FP Langcliffe 1) and cross field to gate/stile at far LH corner. Turn R to descend well-trodden path, passing a cairn to reach a small gate. With a big quarry over on the R, the path swings L and drops to gate in crosswall. Forward with wall on L to enter walled track. ⑩▶ At Langcliffe take middle of three tracks. Turn R at War Memorial then R along main road. ⑪▶ Cross railway and turn L down lane. Cross river footbridge and turn R to stile (FP Stainforth Br 1·5 M). Follow obvious riverside path through a series of stiles. ⑫▶ After passing some hawthorns drop down (FP sign) to river bank. Keep R of gate to ladder-stile beyond and continue upstream. Turn R over bridge and up lane, then R again at main road.

Undulating and moderately strenuous as far as Winskill; thereafter very easy. The section between Tongue Gill and Catrigg Force calls for some careful route-finding. From Catrigg onwards the walk is mostly on very clear paths and tracks. ¾ mile on motor-roads. 1¾ miles of riverside walking. 18 ladder-stiles (8 with adjacent gates). A beautiful walk taking in Craven's most spectacular waterfall and one of the Ribble's loveliest bridges.

STAINFORTH

THERE ARE TWO STAINFORTHS, SEPARATED BY ROAD, RAILWAY AND RIVER. TO THE WEST OF THESE LIES LITTLE STAINFORTH, ORIGINALLY CALLED KNIGHTS STAINFORD. TO THE EAST IS THE MUCH LARGER STAINFORTH, FORMERLY KNOWN AS FRIARS STAINFORD. IT IS AN ATTRACTIVE PLACE OF OLD GREY COTTAGES CLUSTERED HAPHAZARDLY AROUND A VILLAGE GREEN. A LINE OF ANCIENT STEPPING-STONES ACROSS THE BOULDERY STREAM IS A PARTICULARLY PICTURESQUE AND MUCH-PHOTOGRAPHED FEATURE. THE CRAVEN HEIFER DATES FROM THE 17TH C., AND ST. PETER'S CHURCH WAS BUILT IN 1842.

CATRIGG FORCE, or 'Foss'*, plunges 60' in two steps into a deep pool. The setting is exquisite, and the waterfall is mightily impressive after heavy rain. The best view is obtained by descending a path to the bottom of the ravine. The area around the top of the fall is dangerous; definitely not a place for larking about.
*'Force' is Dales dialect for waterfall from the Norse 'Foss'.

TONGUE GILL flows through a remarkably deep ravine, from the hidden depths of which comes the music of tinkling waterfalls. Only one will be seen – at the ravine's upper end.

The Paper Mill

A ghastly blemish on an otherwise flawless riverscape

LANGCLIFFE
is a tranquil place now, but has seen more turbulent times. The original medieval settlement, which belonged to Sawley Abbey and stood about half-a-mile N of the present village, was destroyed by marauding Scots in 1318. Langcliffe Hall, an elegant mansion, has a splendid doorway dated 1602, though the house itself is not as old as that. Look out for a house bearing a tablet displaying a naked woman – with a 1660 date strategically positioned. Perhaps she was the girlfriend of Settle's more famous but equally bashful naked man (see Walk 11).

stile at point ⑨

STAINFORTH FORCE AND BRIDGE
are the highlights of a delightful stroll along the riverbank. Here the Ribble cascades over a series of wide limestone ledges into a big black pool. The graceful bridge was built in the 1670s by Samuel Watson, of nearby Knights Stainford Hall. It is a typical packhorse bridge – very narrow and with low parapets designed so as not to obstruct the panniers slung over the horse's back.

9 GIGGLESWICK SCAR — 5½ MILES

ROUTE DIRECTIONS

① Walk down lane to Giggleswick. ② At T-junction turn L. Pass church and at junction go L up to main road. Walk R along it. ③ Just before reaching bridge turn L along path between fence and wall. Follow it around two L bends to wall-stile. ④ Straight on across field to stile and continue forward alongside wall/fence on L. In next open field bear slightly L to stile into lane. ⑤ Cross lane to stile, turn R in field to walk alongside lane, then bear L (SP Feizor) up rough track. Follow it to a guidepost. ⑥ Turn L (SP Feizor) and climb LH of two paths to crosswall with choice of two ladder-stiles. Straight on up next field to LH of two gateways. ⑦ Swing L up clear, green path which curves L then R before levelling out. Pass to L of wall-corner, through gateway and follow path close to wall on R. ⑧ Near corner of field go through gate and turn L to another gate. Keep straight on along obvious path. ⑨ At guidepost (which may be 'armless') turn sharp L along broad, green path to gate/ladder-stile in wall-corner. Forward with wall on R. At wall-corner keep straight on across field to gate/ladder-stile. Maintain direction to pass through two small gates. ⑩ From second gate follow direction of finger-post (FP Giggleswick). On nearing wall swing L and head for ladder-stile. Keep to the broad path, ignoring any lesser paths branching R. (See notes on 'THE CAVES' on next page). ⑪ Fork L (FP sign) at guidepost. Follow path with a few marker-posts, eventually turning R to descend between old wall and fence, with a huge quarry on the R. Keep to path alongside quarry fence, turning R with it at far end of quarry. ⑫ Go through tall iron gate and descend steeply (care needed in wet conditions). Don't use the quarry access road – a thin path (may be a bit overgrown) winds down through woodland to the road. Turn R then L down lane past golf course.

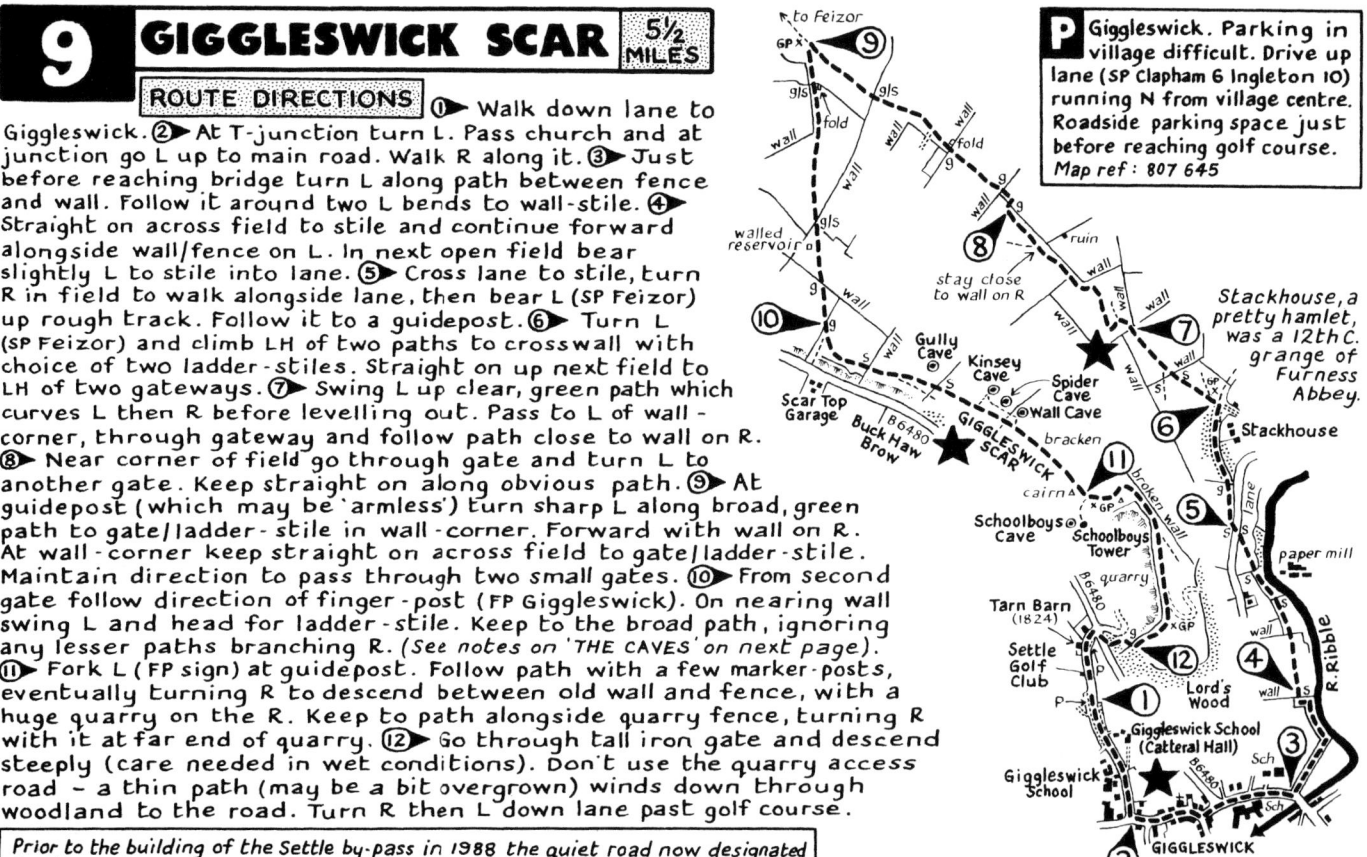

P Giggleswick. Parking in village difficult. Drive up lane (SP Clapham 6 Ingleton 10) running N from village centre. Roadside parking space just before reaching golf course. Map ref : 807 645

Stackhouse, a pretty hamlet, was a 12th C. grange of Furness Abbey.

Prior to the building of the Settle by-pass in 1988 the quiet road now designated B6480 was the main A65, and heaving with traffic. It follows the line of a major geological fault (very evident at Buck Haw (pron. 'Bucka') Brow), with dramatic limestone scenery to its NE and somewhat dreary gritstone plains to its SW.

NOTE: LIMESTONE SCARS AND CLINTS OMITTED FROM THE MAP FOR THE SAKE OF CLARITY

Surprisingly easy walking on good, dry paths through limestone pastures. A charming village and some interesting caves. Less than a mile on motor-roads. 6 ladder-stiles (3 with adjacent gates). Lots of sheep, so dogs will probably have to be kept on lead for much of the time.

GIGGLESWICK
VILLAGE, CHURCH AND SCHOOL

The somewhat whimsical name, which seldom fails to raise a chuckle, is from the Norse 'wic' (a village) and 'Gikel' or 'Gigel' (a chieftain of around the 10th C.). It is a delectable place, full of pretty 17th C cottages clustered haphazardly around quaint little nooks and crannies. Tems Beck, a little stream known affectionately by the locals as 'the River Tems', passes under a series of tiny bridges as it makes its way merrily through the heart of the village. Giggleswick School is a famous and highly reputable seat of learning founded in the early years of the 16th C by local benefactor James Carr of Stackhouse. A landmark for miles around is the 98' high copper dome of the school chapel, built in 1901. The lovely church is dedicated to St. Akelda, a rather obscure Saxon Christian who is thought to have been strangled for her faith. Earliest records of the building date from the reign of Stephen (1135-54). In 1318 the church suffered a battering at the hands of invading Scots, and the 15th C. tower may well have been erected for defensive purposes. The interior has some very fine 17th C. woodwork, including pulpit, reading-desk, communion rails and poor box. A notable feature is the tomb of Sir Richard Tempest, a Lancastrian stalwart in the Wars of the Roses, who was knighted at the Battle of Wakefield 1460. It is said that his tomb contains the skull of his beloved warhorse.

THE CAVES

GULLY CAVE, at the head of a dry gully, is a complete fraud. It looks impressive from below, and many a walker must have made the rough climb up scree and boulders only to find that it is merely a shallow alcove in the rock face. KINSEY CAVE is identically situated in another dry valley, but cannot be seen from below. To reach it, cross the valley and turn L up a thin path to the 8' high by 25' wide mouth of a cave which has yielded evidence of occupation by prehistoric man, various animal bones and a cave bear's skull. On returning from the cave, turn L around the base of the scar to locate SPIDER CAVE, whilst a little further on, just beyond a ruined wall, is WALL CAVE. To visit SCHOOLBOYS CAVE, detour R at point ⑪ to the massive circular cairn known as Schoolboys Tower. The cave is about 40 yards to its W, at the base of the upper scar, but may take some finding, as its entrance is concealed by an elderberry tree. All these caves are safe to enter, and make snug refuges in showery weather.

Kinsey Cave

In summer on the limestone uplands look out for the dainty WHEATEAR, with its flashing white rump and grating 'chack chack' call. The handsome male is cream and grey, with black cheek-stripes.

THE PRESENT GOLF COURSE OCCUPIES THE SITE OF A FORMER TARN (note Tarn Barn 1824). THIS CONSIDERABLE SHEET OF WATER, SOME ¾ MILE LONG, 100 YARDS WIDE AND ABOUT 12' DEEP WAS DRAINED IN 1830, AND WHEN THE LAND WAS CULTIVATED 33 YEARS LATER LABOURERS UNEARTHED A BRONZE AGE FISHERMAN'S CANOE. THE BOAT WAS DISPLAYED IN LEEDS MUSEUM UNTIL WORLD WAR II, WHEN IT WAS DESTROYED BY THE DASTARDLY LUFTWAFFE.

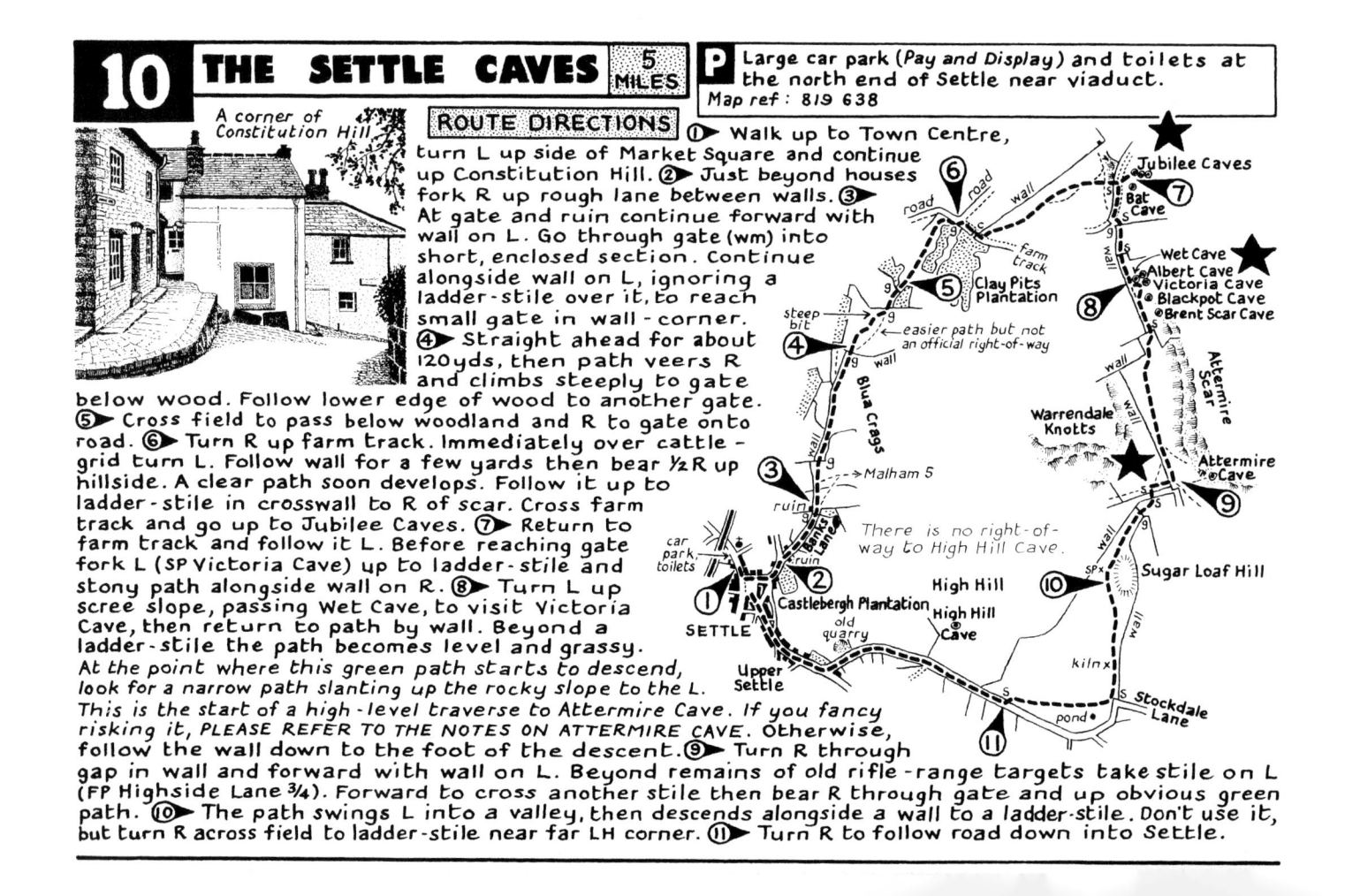

10 THE SETTLE CAVES 5 MILES

P Large car park (Pay and Display) and toilets at the north end of Settle near viaduct. Map ref : 819 638

A corner of Constitution Hill

ROUTE DIRECTIONS

① Walk up to Town Centre, turn L up side of Market Square and continue up Constitution Hill. ② Just beyond houses fork R up rough lane between walls. ③ At gate and ruin continue forward with wall on L. Go through gate (wm) into short, enclosed section. Continue alongside wall on L, ignoring a ladder-stile over it, to reach small gate in wall-corner. ④ Straight ahead for about 120yds, then path veers R and climbs steeply to gate below wood. Follow lower edge of wood to another gate. ⑤ Cross field to pass below woodland and R to gate onto road. ⑥ Turn R up farm track. Immediately over cattle-grid turn L. Follow wall for a few yards then bear ½R up hillside. A clear path soon develops. Follow it up to ladder-stile in crosswall to R of scar. Cross farm track and go up to Jubilee Caves. ⑦ Return to farm track and follow it L. Before reaching gate fork L (SP Victoria Cave) up to ladder-stile and stony path alongside wall on R. ⑧ Turn L up scree slope, passing Wet Cave, to visit Victoria Cave, then return to path by wall. Beyond a ladder-stile the path becomes level and grassy. At the point where this green path starts to descend, look for a narrow path slanting up the rocky slope to the L. This is the start of a high-level traverse to Attermire Cave. If you fancy risking it, PLEASE REFER TO THE NOTES ON ATTERMIRE CAVE. Otherwise, follow the wall down to the foot of the descent. ⑨ Turn R through gap in wall and forward with wall on L. Beyond remains of old rifle-range targets take stile on L (FP Highside Lane ¾). Forward to cross another stile then bear R through gate and up obvious green path. ⑩ The path swings L into a valley, then descends alongside a wall to a ladder-stile. Don't use it, but turn R across field to ladder-stile near far LH corner. ⑪ Turn R to follow road down into Settle.

Jubilee Caves
Bat Cave
Wet Cave
Albert Cave
Victoria Cave
Blackpot Cave
Brent Scar Cave
Attermire Scar
Warrendale Knotts
Attermire Cave
Clay Pits Plantation
easier path but not an official right-of-way
steep bit
Blua Crags
→ Malham 5
ruin
car park toilets
Banks Lane
There is no right-of-way to High Hill Cave.
Sugar Loaf Hill
High Hill
High Hill Cave
Castleberg Plantation
old quarry
SETTLE
Upper Settle
kiln x
Stockdale Lane
pond

Moderately strenuous, but almost entirely on clear paths over firm, dry, limestone pastures. The wallside path below the caves, however, is rough and slippery, and should be trodden circumspectly. 5 ladder-stiles. 1 mile on motor-roads. A walk of exceptional beauty and interest through some of the finest limestone scenery in the Dales.

10

JUBILEE CAVES

There are three entrances—the two illustrated and another round to the R. Excavations within the caves have unearthed the remains of numerous Iron Age burials. Most of the skeletons were found secreted in recesses along the sides of narrow inner passages; one was wearing a necklace made from the teeth of a wolf.

BAT CAVE is a short (10') cave situated at the foot of a scar about 60 yds S of Jubilee Caves.

Just beyond Victoria Cave we pass two more prominent caves. **BLACKPOT CAVE** lies at the base of the lower scar, and **BRENT SCAR CAVE** is a high, vertical fissure above a scree slope.

The area of limestone tors to our right is called **WARRENDALE KNOTTS**. There is a fine view of these jagged and splintered outcrops from the stile just beyond point ⑨.

VICTORIA CAVE

YOU ARE MOST STRONGLY WARNED NOT TO GO INTO VICTORIA CAVE OR NEAR TO THE ENTRANCE. THERE HAVE BEEN SERIOUS ROCK FALLS. THE AUTHORITY ACCEPTS NO RESPONSIBILITY FOR ANY INJURY OR DAMAGE.

Victoria Cave was so named because it was discovered in 1837, the year of Victoria's coronation. The huge entrance (40' high and 100' wide) is artificial—the result of extensive excavations which have unearthed a wealth of archaeological remains. Romano-British artefacts (3rd and 4thC) were found in the uppermost layers of the cave floor. Below these was a 6' deposit of sediment and cave debris indicating a long period of disuse. Deeper still were found Stone Age implements and, in a pre-Ice Age layer, the bones of grizzly bear, reindeer, hyena, rhinoceros, hippopotamus, elephant and wild ox. Some of these bones were estimated to have been at least 120,000 years old.

ALBERT CAVE is above, and 70 yards to the L of, Victoria Cave.

WET CAVE can be entered and explored for about 50', but it's a bit drippy and slimy, as its name would suggest.

ATTERMIRE CAVE

The high-level path to the cave needs care, and is not suitable for very young children. Just before the path reaches the base of a cliff turn very sharp L to make a short, zig-zag climb up the rocks to a grassy ledge leading to the cave. Note the abundance of snails hereabouts. With two good torches one can walk along a winding passage for about 60'. If you have more bottle (or less sense) than the author, and no regard for the state of your kit, you can then crawl for 20' to emerge into a large chamber containing a knee-deep pool. On leaving the cave return to the foot of the 'zig-zag' and go straight down the steep slope to the wall-gap at point ⑨.

FOR NOTES ON SETTLE SEE WALK 11

P Large car park *(Pay and Display)* and toilets at the north end of Settle near viaduct.
Map ref: 819 638

ROUTE DIRECTIONS

① Walk up to town centre and take road signposted 'Upper Settle, Malham, Airton. Pass The Folly and up Victoria Street. ② At Chapel House fork R ('no through road' sign). ③ 80yds past water treatment works take gate on R (FP Mitchell Lane ½ M). Follow wall on R, crossing to other side of it at a gate. ④ Just before top corner of field take wall-stile/gate on L. Bear R around far side of outcrops up to stile in crosswall. Turn L to follow wall. ⑤ Cross ladder-stile at top corner and turn sharp R (BW Turnpike House) along walled track. Go L at junction of tracks. ⑥ Don't enter farmyard but turn L up to gate and forward with wall on R. At wall-corner keep straight ahead past a solitary tree to climb to wall-stile into wood. ⑦ Clear path winds down through wood. Approaching edge of wood the path swings R (ignore small footbridge down on L). ⑧ Leaving the wood at a gate, turn R and R again through gap in wall to follow wall on R, eventually heading for group of barns via series of stiles. ⑨ Turn L along farm road, cross road and down another farm road to river. ⑩ Just before by-pass bridge go through gate on L. Cross by-pass bridge, turn sharp R down to ladder-stile, then turn L upstream (FP Giggleswick). Keep to riverside. ⑪ From gate/stile (where river bends R) keep straight on (towards a tall, thin chimney) to reach swing-gate. Cross to tarmac path between two bungalows. On emerging into modern housing estate go straight across to path (RW sign) to L of Nº 36 leading to stile in corner. ⑫ Forward along RH edge of field. Go R through stile and follow riverside path. ⑬ Cross footbridge and along road. Go L at Y-junction and R at next junction. Straight on under railway to town centre.

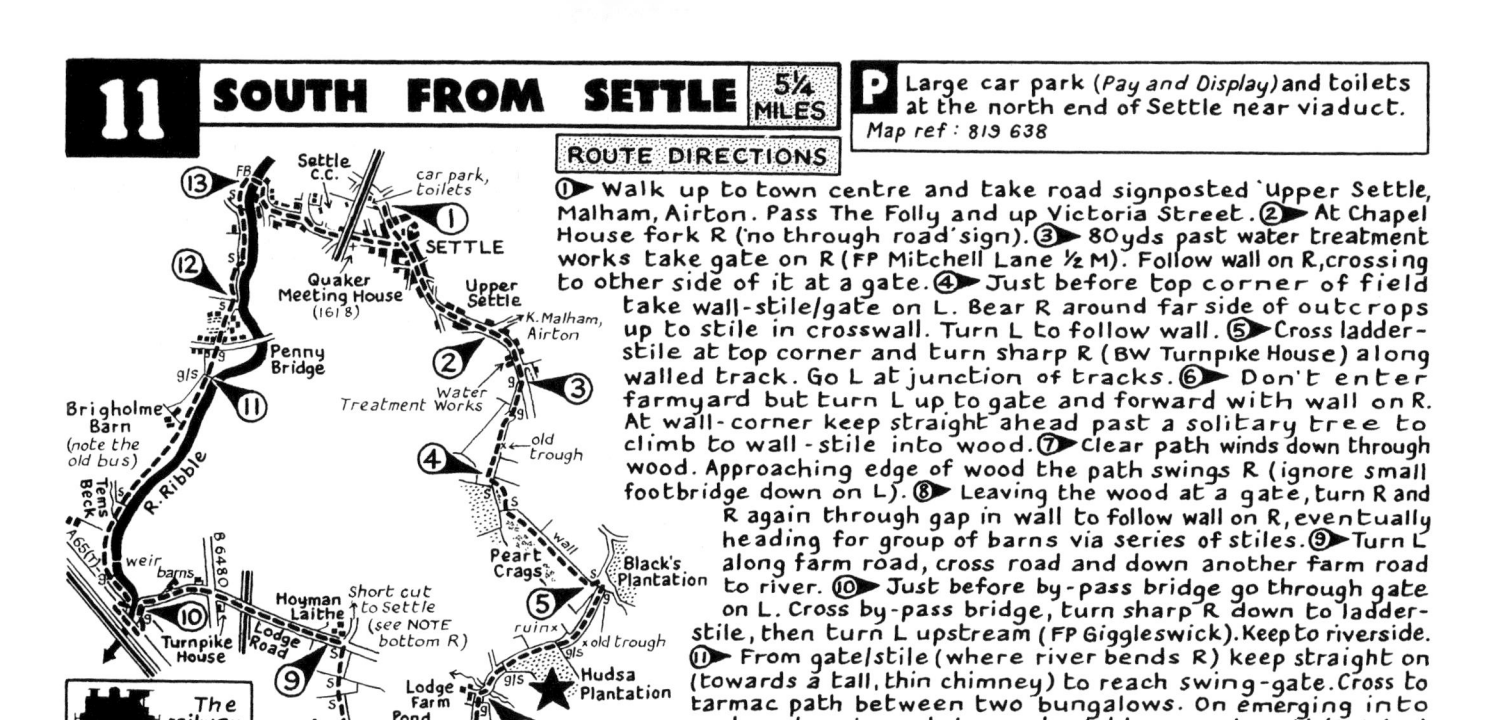

Brigholme Barn *(note the old bus)*

The railway passing under Lodge Road is the famous Settle-Carlisle line, whilst the one alongside the A65(T) Settle by-pass runs to Lancaster. The lines converge at Settle Junction, half-a-mile SW of Cleatop Park.

SETTLE
Twinned with BANYULS SUR MER

NOTE: Anyone in a desperate hurry, dying of thirst, powfagged *, soaked to the skin or brassed-off may make a quick and direct return to Settle by taking the walled track (FP Settle) to the R of the barns at point ⑨.
* Lancashire word - synonym of knackered.

First half of walk, as far as Cleatop Park, is undulating, with about 525' of ascent. Thereafter the going is extremely easy. Varied terrain includes pathless pastures, a delectable walkers' track (between Black's and Hudsa Plantations), farm roads, some exquisite woodland, a mile of riverside walking and ¾ mile on motor-roads. 5 ladder-stiles (4 with adjacent gates). Best in late Spring/early Summer (for rhododendrons and woodland flowers).

SETTLE

SETTLE is a lively little town clinging to the steep hillsides and overlooked by the towering limestone cliffs of CASTLEBERG (depicted in the sign on the left). Recorded as 'Setel' in the Domesday Book, and granted a market charter in 1249, Settle is a fascinating, higgledy-piggledy hotchpotch of narrow alleys, steep lanes and picturesque old courtyards, with here and there some fine Georgian town-houses. In the MARKET SQUARE the prominent, arch-fronted building is called THE SHAMBLES - built in the 17th C. and originally an open market hall. The arches and cottages were added during the late 18th C.,

Ye Olde Naked Man

1668

CLEATOP PARK

Better-known as Cleatop Wood

This patch of ancient and richly colourful woodland is owned by the National Park and designated as a Site of Special Scientific Interest. An extensive range of woodland plants can be found here, and the wide variety of trees includes oak, beech, birch, pine and larch. From the gate at the bottom of the wood there is a fine view across Ribblesdale to Lancashire's dark, heathery Bowland Fells.

and around 1898 the cottages were given an upper storey. Across the Square stands YE OLDE NAKED MAN CAFE, formerly an inn and so named from the relief figure of a man modestly hiding his credentials behind a 1668 datestone. In Victoria Street we pass a huge, Tudor-style house with an ornate central doorway and fine Jacobean windows. Known as THE FOLLY, it was built in 1675 for Thomas Preston, a wealthy tanner (hence its alternative name of Tanner Hall). UPPER SETTLE is the oldest part of the town, and has some attractive little groups of 17th. and 18th C. cottages.

Upon re-entering the town, and before reaching the railway bridge, pop through the gate on the L to have a look at the CRICKET GROUND, with its attractive and unusual backdrop of dark viaduct and gleaming limestone fells. Settle C.C. plays in the Ribblesdale League. Just under the bridge on the R is the FRIENDS' MEETING HOUSE, which dates from 1689. Across the road is VICTORIA HALL, built in 1853 as a music hall.

Turnpike House

Once a toll-house on the Keighley-Kendal turnpike road. The turnpike road was built in the mid-18th C.

Porch - Friends' Meeting House

12 THE INGS OF RIBBLE 7¼ MILES

P Rathmell. Small car park adjacent to village Reading Room. Map ref: 804 600

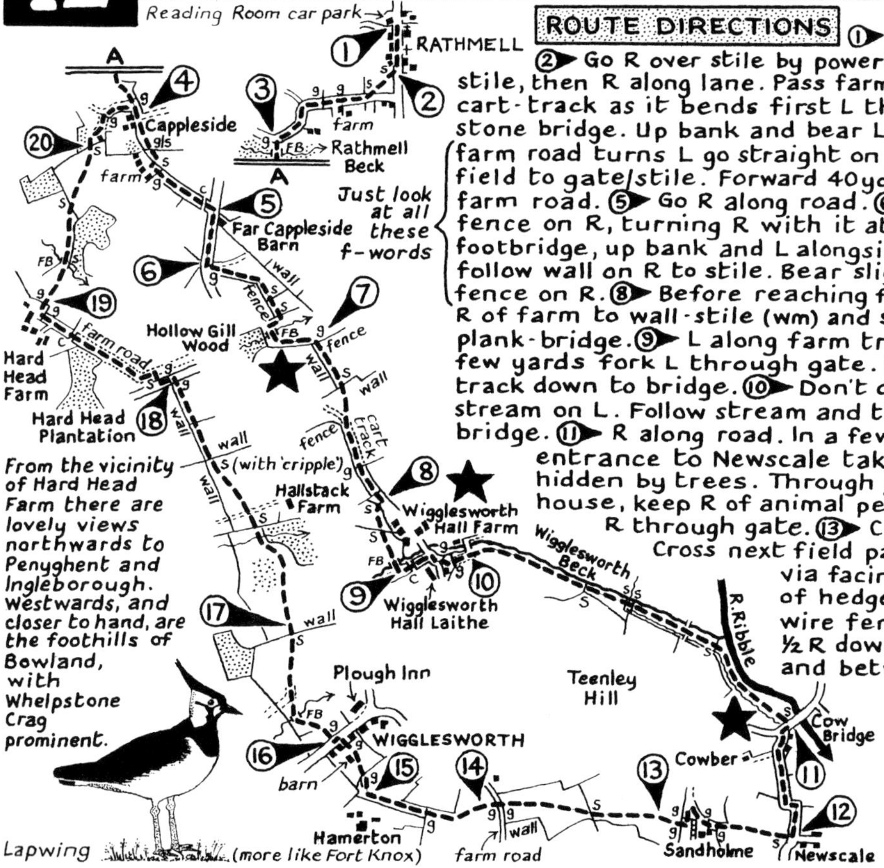

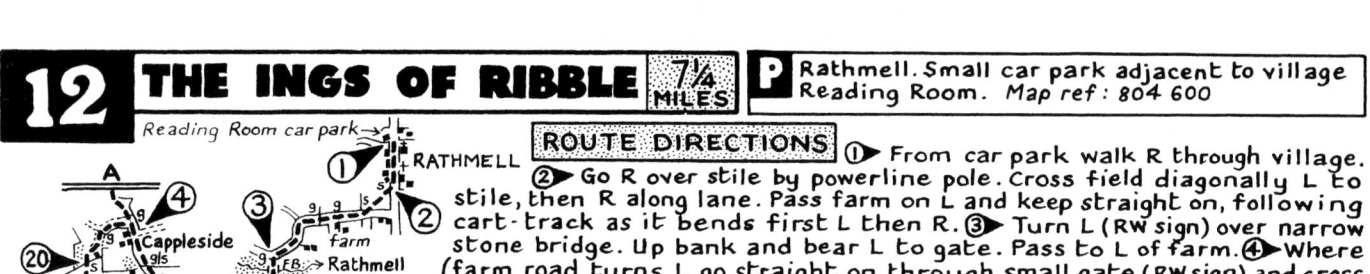

Reading Room car park

RATHMELL

Cappleside

Rathmell Beck

A

Just look at all these f-words

Far Cappleside Barn

Hollow Gill Wood

Hard Head Farm

Hard Head Plantation

From the vicinity of Hard Head Farm there are lovely views northwards to Penyghent and Ingleborough. Westwards, and closer to hand, are the foothills of Bowland, with Whelpstone Crag prominent.

Hallstack Farm

Wigglesworth Hall Farm

Wigglesworth Hall Laithe

Wigglesworth Beck

Plough Inn

Teenley Hill

R. Ribble

WIGGLESWORTH

barn

Hamerton (more like Fort Knox)

farm road

Sandholme

Cowber

Cow Bridge

Newscale

Lapwing

ROUTE DIRECTIONS

① From car park walk R through village. ② Go R over stile by powerline pole. Cross field diagonally L to stile, then R along lane. Pass farm on L and keep straight on, following cart-track as it bends first L then R. ③ Turn L (RW sign) over narrow stone bridge. Up bank and bear L to gate. Pass to L of farm. ④ Where farm road turns L go straight on through small gate (RW sign) and cross field to gate/stile. Forward 40yds to stile into farmyard and out along farm road. ⑤ Go R along road. ⑥ Turn L through gate (RW sign). Follow fence on R, turning R with it at corner (RW sign). At stream turn R to footbridge, up bank and L alongside fence. ⑦ Take LH of 2 gates and follow wall on R to stile. Bear slightly R to locate cart-track (wm) with fence on R. ⑧ Before reaching farm take wooden stile (wm) on R. Keep R of farm to wall-stile (wm) and stay parallel with buildings to cross plank-bridge. ⑨ L along farm track. At T-junction turn R and in a few yards fork L through gate. Go L through another gate to follow track down to bridge. ⑩ Don't cross bridge. Keep straight on, with stream on L. Follow stream and then Ribble to stile at RH end of road bridge. ⑪ R along road. In a few yards L (RW sign) up lane. ⑫ At the entrance to Newscale take stile on R. Aim for buildings partially hidden by trees. Through gate to enclosed track. Cross lawn of house, keep R of animal pens then turn sharp L behind them and R through gate. ⑬ Cross field to stile at LH end of crosswall. Cross next field passing R of wall-corner. Cross farm road via facing gates. ⑭ Straight on, passing L of hedge-corner to gate into track with high wire fence on L. ⑮ At wm on high fence go ½ R down to small handgate. Pass R of barn and between houses to road. ⑯ Go 30yds L along road to gate (FP sign) and down field to footbridge at LH corner. Ascend cart-track, and when it peters out keep straight on to broken-down stile by powerline pole. ⑰ Go forward between 2 woods and round top end of the one on the R to stile. Cross

A peaceful and pleasant ramble, mostly through fairly level, pathless pastures, in a section of Ribblesdale somewhat neglected by walkers. The going is easy, but finding the way is *not*, so consult the oracle carefully. The route is liberally sprinkled with waymarks except, of course, in the places where they are most needed. 2 ladder-stiles. Only 1/3 mile on motor-roads. Expect glutinous mud in wet weather.

next field to stile at LH corner and forward with wall on L. ⑱► L up green track. In 60yds cross stile on R and go L up farm road. ⑲► Enter farmyard and turn R through gate. Cross field to footbridge (wonky) and climb alongside wood to stile in crosswall. Follow powerline to another stile. ⑳► Keep L through garden, pass L of house and along narrow path to gate. Follow rough lane to R. Go L through gate (wm) and down to bridge at point ③. Retrace outward route.

THE INGS OF RIBBLE

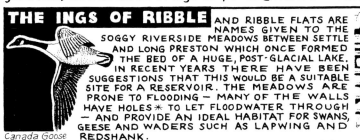

Canada Goose

AND RIBBLE FLATS ARE NAMES GIVEN TO THE SOGGY RIVERSIDE MEADOWS BETWEEN SETTLE AND LONG PRESTON WHICH ONCE FORMED THE BED OF A HUGE, POST-GLACIAL LAKE. IN RECENT YEARS THERE HAVE BEEN SUGGESTIONS THAT THIS WOULD BE A SUITABLE SITE FOR A RESERVOIR. THE MEADOWS ARE PRONE TO FLOODING — MANY OF THE WALLS HAVE HOLES * TO LET FLOODWATER THROUGH — AND PROVIDE AN IDEAL HABITAT FOR SWANS, GEESE AND WADERS SUCH AS LAPWING AND REDSHANK.

A Creep Hole

*Another type of hole-in-wall is the Creep Hole, or 'Cripple', which allows sheep to pass between fields. Cripples are common throughout the Dales, and there is a good example by a stile on the way up to Hard Head Farm.

Rathmell Reading Room

RATHMELL is a sleepy little village with no pretension to beauty but with an undeniable rustic charm. One feels that here time is measured in centuries rather than days. Holy Trinity Church is worth visiting for its lovely stained glass windows. In 1670 the Reverend Richard Frankland founded a college at Rathmell for the training of nonconformist ministers. Frankland's 'Academy' was the first of its kind in the country, but it incurred the wrath of the church authorities to such a degree that they excommunicated him. Frankland died in 1698 and is buried in Giggleswick church.

WIGGLESWORTH HALL was once a grange of Fountains Abbey, and the buildings still contain fragments of monastic remains. 200yds S of the Hall is a barn 165' long — one of the largest in Britain. It was severely fire-damaged in 1958 and subsequently re-roofed.

The celebrated Plough

Apart from the very striking Plough Inn, the village of **WIGGLESWORTH** is fairly unremarkable, but things might have been different. Because of the presence of sulphur in the streams hereabouts, there were once plans to build a spa town here to rival Harrogate. In another grandiose and soon-abandoned scheme, the Settle Mining Co, in 1868, sank a shaft in search of coal.

13 LONG PRESTON — 6 MILES

P Long Preston. There is space to park by the village green. Map ref : 834 582

ROUTE DIRECTIONS

①► Start along lane (School Lane) behind green. Just past school **turn L** (FP Langber Lane 1½ M) along farm lane. Where it turns L to farm keep straight on along walled track to cross footbridge. **②►** Pass to R of walled reservoir and climb field to stile at top LH corner. Cross corner of field to ladder-stile and up next field to ladder-stile on skyline. **③►** Turn L up field. When ruined building appears make a beeline for it. Pass L of ruin, via ladder-stiles, to reach walled track. **④►** Go R for a few yards, then L through gate/ladder-stile (FP Kirkby Malham 3 M). Forward alongside wall to stile in crosswall about 80yds from corner. Keep straight on, aiming towards highest point of skyline. **⑤►** Go through gate/stile in crosswall and head for buildings. Pass to L of RH building and turn R along farm road. **⑥►** Cross cattle-grid then bear L off farm road and follow powerlines down two fields (ignore green path forking R in 2nd field). Over stile in crosswall and turn R down to farm track. **⑦►** Turn R over cattle-grid and along farm road. When wall ends go through gate and diagonally R across field to stile. Maintain direction, aiming towards LH end of band of trees, to reach gate/stile in bottom corner. **⑧►** Ford stream. From guidepost take path climbing steep hillside (FP Long Preston 1¾). At top continue past wall-corner then drop to gate/ladder-stile. **⑨►** Cross track to ladder-stile. Follow direction of fingerpost (FP Long Preston 1½) across field then drop to stile in crosswall about 80yds from valley on L. Turn L to follow wall to footbridge/stile. **⑩►** Turn R and get onto high ground to locate thin path. Follow it downstream. **⑪►** Approaching crosswall fork R to stile. Continue downstream. **⑫►** Cross bridge to gate (wm) into farmyard. Turn R through series of gates and along farm lane. **⑬►** Fork R along walled path to re-join outward route near school.

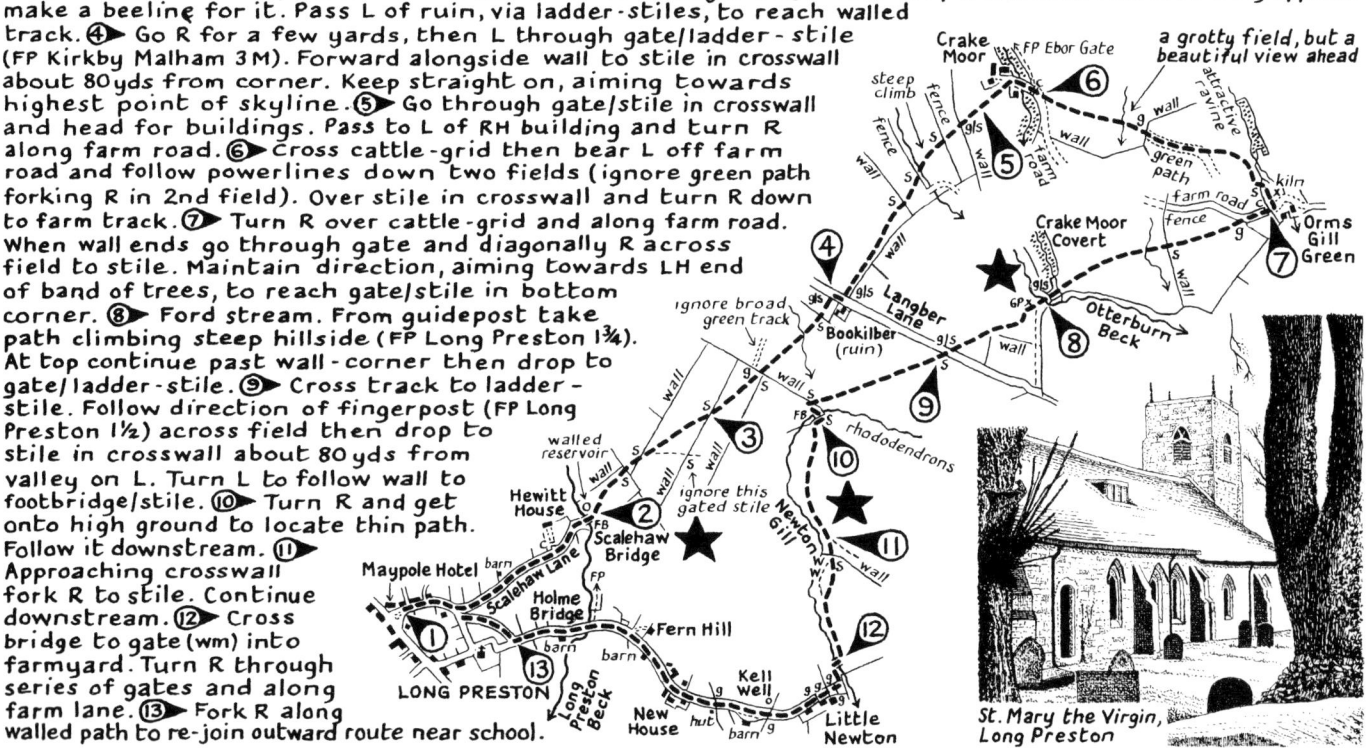

St. Mary the Virgin, Long Preston

A fairly strenuous journey over lonely, rolling, windswept sheep pastures with some quite outstanding views. Much of the route is pathless, and the walk should be avoided in mist, when the section between Orms Gill Green and Newton Gill would be particularly irksome. Motor-road walking negligible. 7 ladder-stiles (3 with adjacent gates). NOTE : If desired, the walk may be reduced to 3¾ miles by nipping along Langber Lane from Bookilber (point ④) to the stile at point ⑨.

LONG PRESTON

It is Long Preston's misfortune to straddle the A65, and thus be blighted by the constant rumble of huge lorries, the pollution of an incessant stream of vehicles and the menace of witless drivers who take scant notice of the speed restrictions. Only a leisurely exploration of Long Preston's back lanes will reveal the village's true character – a charming mélange of pretty cottages and busy working farms.

THE BEAUTIFUL AND SURPRISINGLY LARGE CHURCH IS ONE OF THE FEW IN CRAVEN TO BE MENTIONED IN THE DOMESDAY BOOK, THOUGH THE PRESENT STRUCTURE DATES BACK ONLY (!) TO THE 14TH C. THE TOWER WAS REBUILT IN 1760 AND THE CHANCEL IN 1868. ABOVE THE PORCH DOORWAY IS AN ANCIENT STONE CROSS, AND THE PORCH WALL INCORPORATES A MEDIEVAL GRAVE SLAB. THE CRUDE HEXAGONAL FONT HAS A FINE JACOBEAN CANOPY DATED 1726, AND THE EXQUISITE PULPIT IS OF THE SAME VINTAGE. ON THE SOUTH SIDE OF THE ALTAR IS THE HAMMERTON TOMB, DATED 1445. THE HAMMERTONS THEN RESIDED AT HELLIFIELD PEEL (See Walk 14). THE CHURCHYARD SUNDIAL DATES FROM 1659.

In the 1920s the site of a Roman camp was discovered on a knoll immediately to the east of the churchyard.

It is a surprise to see **RHODODENDRONS** flourishing in the upper ravine of Newton Gill. The wild rhododendron (Rh. ponticum) is an unusual feature in limestone country, preferring a more acidic, peaty soil.

YOU MAY BE LUCKY ENOUGH TO SEE **RED DEER** AT LITTLE NEWTON, FOR THE FARMER KEEPS A SMALL HERD (A STAG AND 4 HINDS). THE STAG IS A NOBLE CREATURE AND SO IT SHOULD BE, FOR IT CAME HERE FROM WOBURN ABBEY.

LONG PRESTON BECK looks fairly innocuous, but like most rivers it has potentially devastating power. In the summer of 1881 a flash flood caused the beck to rampage through the village, causing widespread damage.

BOOKILBER

Never in all his wanderings has the author encountered a more dismal place than this. On the 19th August 1996 the house was gutted by a fire in which a woman tragically lost her life. An aura of gloom and desolation still hangs over the sombre ruins of Bookilber.

ORMS GILL GREEN FARM

is notable for its large limekiln. In the mid-18th C. Dales farmers began to build intake walls to enclose land on the edge of the moors. The new fields needed to be limed, and kilns were constructed to produce the huge amounts required.

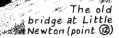

The old bridge at Little Newton (point ⑫)

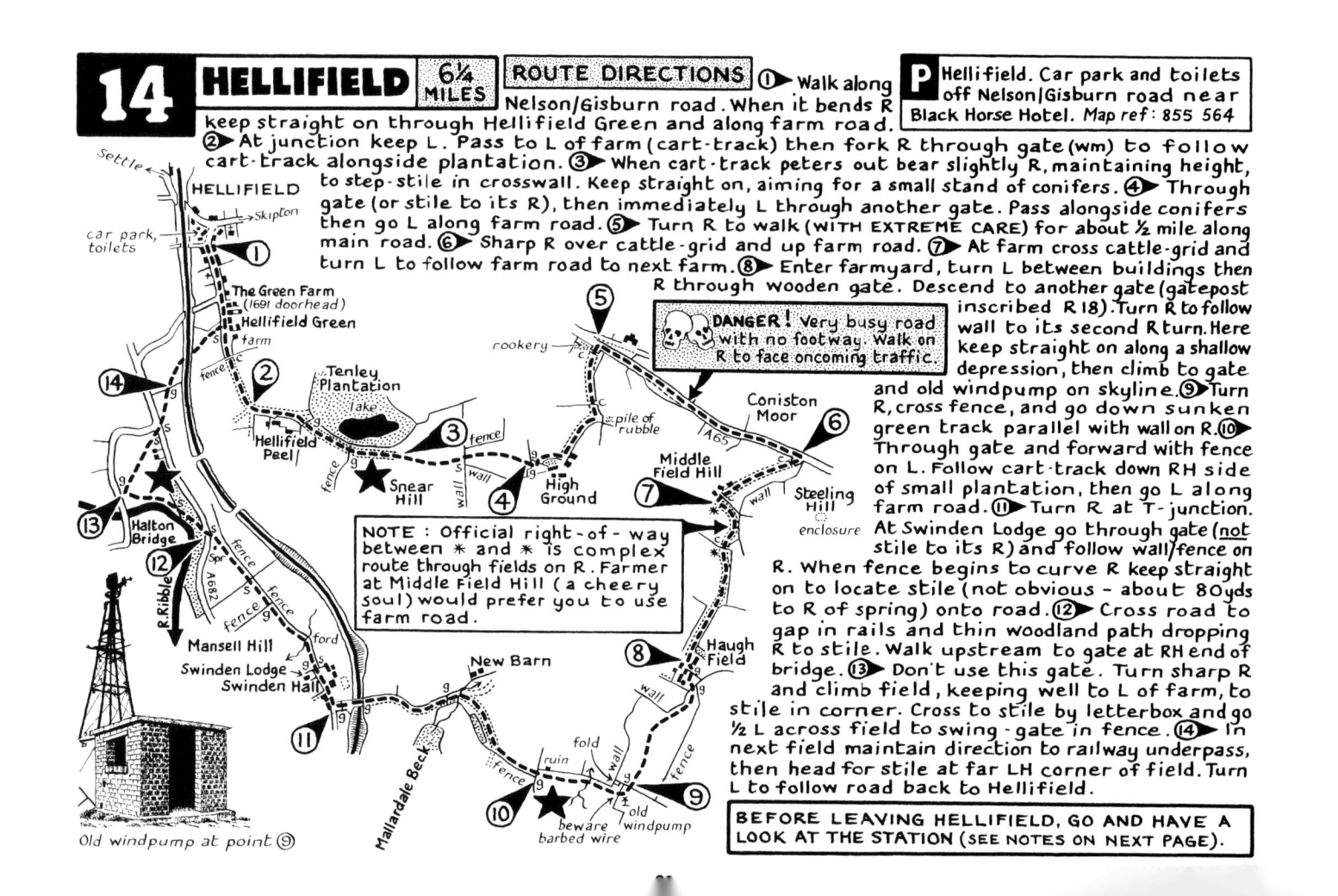

14 HELLIFIELD 6¼ MILES

ROUTE DIRECTIONS

① Walk along Nelson/Gisburn road. When it bends R keep straight on through Hellifield Green and along farm road. **②** At junction keep L. Pass to L of farm (cart-track) then fork R through gate (wm) to follow cart-track alongside plantation. **③** When cart-track peters out bear slightly R, maintaining height, to step-stile in crosswall. Keep straight on, aiming for a small stand of conifers. **④** Through gate (or stile to its R), then immediately L through another gate. Pass alongside conifers then go L along farm road. **⑤** Turn R to walk (WITH EXTREME CARE) for about ½ mile along main road. **⑥** Sharp R over cattle-grid and up farm road. **⑦** At farm cross cattle-grid and turn L to follow farm road to next farm. **⑧** Enter farmyard, turn L between buildings then R through wooden gate. Descend to another gate (gatepost inscribed R18). Turn R to follow wall to its second R turn. Here keep straight on along a shallow depression, then climb to gate and old windpump on skyline. **⑨** Turn R, cross fence, and go down sunken green track parallel with wall on R. **⑩** Through gate and forward with fence on L. Follow cart-track down RH side of small plantation, then go L along farm road. **⑪** Turn R at T-junction. At Swinden Lodge go through gate (not stile to its R) and follow wall/fence on R. When fence begins to curve R keep straight on to locate stile (not obvious – about 80yds to R of spring) onto road. **⑫** Cross road to gap in rails and thin woodland path dropping R to stile. Walk upstream to gate at RH end of bridge. **⑬** Don't use this gate. Turn sharp R and climb field, keeping well to L of farm, to stile in corner. Cross to stile by letterbox and go ½ L across field to swing-gate in fence. **⑭** In next field maintain direction to railway underpass, then head for stile at far LH corner of field. Turn L to follow road back to Hellifield.

P Hellifield. Car park and toilets off Nelson/Gisburn road near Black Horse Hotel. Map ref: 855 564

DANGER! Very busy road with no footway. Walk on R to face oncoming traffic.

NOTE: Official right-of-way between ★ and ★ is complex route through fields on R. Farmer at Middle Field Hill (a cheery soul) would prefer you to use farm road.

BEFORE LEAVING HELLIFIELD, GO AND HAVE A LOOK AT THE STATION (SEE NOTES ON NEXT PAGE).

Map labels: Settle, HELLIFIELD, Skipton, car park toilets, The Green Farm (1691 doorhead), Hellifield Green farm, Tenley Plantation, lake, Hellifield Peel, Snear Hill, High Ground, rookery, pile of rubble, Coniston Moor, A65, Middle Field Hill, Steeling Hill, enclosure, Haugh Field, New Barn, Halton Bridge, R. Ribble, A682, Mansell Hill, Swinden Lodge, Swinden Hall, ford, Mallardale Beck, fold, ruin, beware barbed wire, old windpump

Old windpump at point ⑨

Easy walking through gently undulating farmland. 1 mile is on motor-roads and 2½ miles on farm roads and cart-tracks. WARNING: THE ROUTE REQUIRES YOU TO UNDERTAKE A DEATH-DEFYING ½ MILE WALK ALONG THE BUSY A65 - DECIDEDLY UNPLEASANT, AND PARTICULARLY AWKWARD WITH A DOG. No ladder-stiles. The route is not well-blessed with waymarks, which would certainly be helpful at High Ground ④ and Haugh Field ⑧.

HELLIFIELD

— a somewhat grey and drab village riven by the busy A65 - is an ancient settlement which pottered along for centuries as a serene and peaceful farming community until its bucolic bliss was blighted by the advent of the railway. Hellifield rose to great prominence as a rail-junction, and on no account should visitors fail to seek out the station. It was built by the Midland Railway Co., and the castings of the canopy — a magnificent example of Victorian ironwork — carry the company's dragon emblem and the initials MR. Its heyday is now long gone but, at the time of writing, the station is being developed into what promises to be a fascinating Visitor Centre (due to open Spring 1998).

The Parish Church, though of no great antiquity, is an attractive and well cared-for building.

Barn door at The Green Farm

On **STEELING HILL** is an oval, ditched earthwork with an entrance to the east. Its origin is uncertain, but there are two theories: a) a small Roman signal station. b) a 10th C. 'lodge' or stockade to protect flocks and herds nocturnally from wolves.

SWINDEN HALL

IS A SUPREMELY LOVELY OLD BUILDING. BUILT IN 1567 - PROBABLY TO REPLACE AN EXISTING HOUSE - THE HALL BELONGED TO THE TALBOT FAMILY OF BASHALL (NEAR CLITHEROE) UNTIL 1660. ABOVE THE DOOR IS A CRUDELY EXECUTED INSCRIPTION - MAYT HE16 EWA NdH W.
A SLIGHT ADJUSTMENT OF SPACING MAKES MORE SENSE - MAY THE 16 EW ANd HW.
50 YARDS SE OF THE HALL, BETWEEN THE HOUSE AND THE RAILWAY, IS THE SITE OF A SMALL ROMAN FORT.

The beautiful 3-storey porch of Swinden Hall

Hellifield Peel as it looked in 1937

de Knolle

Hamerton

This once-noble house is now a sad sight indeed - a crumbling, overgrown, forlorn ruin bristling with 'Keep Out' signs. The house was built by the de Knoll family, and was their home until the latter years of the reign of Edward III (1327-77). The oldest remaining part is a rectangular block at the east end, which was constructed as a solar tower in the 14th C. The house was fortified to resist attacks by marauding Scots, which were a common occurence in 14th C. Northern England. It was encircled by a moat, remains of which can be clearly seen. Ownership of the Peel passed from the de Knolls to the Hammertons, and in 1536 Sir Stephen of that ilk landed himself in serious bother by getting involved in the Pilgrimage of Grace. He was duly hanged and beheaded at Tyburn on 25th May 1537. Local tradition claims that the Peel has an underground passage connecting with Wigglesworth Hall, but this is a bit hard to swallow; the two houses are over three miles apart! The Peel was occupied by the Hammertons until 1948, and was partially demolished in 1954.

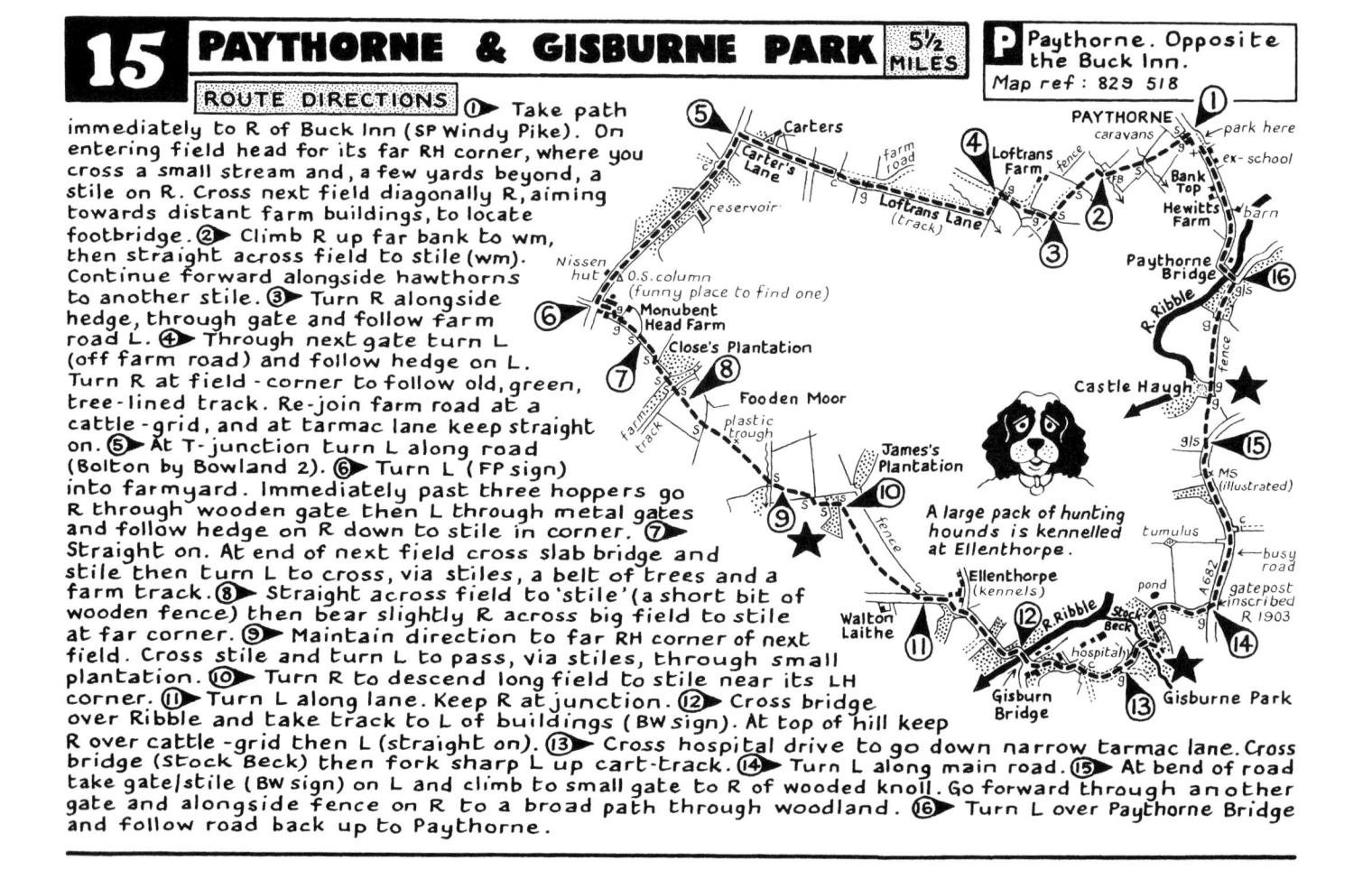

15 PAYTHORNE & GISBURNE PARK 5½ MILES

P Paythorne. Opposite the Buck Inn. Map ref: 829 518

ROUTE DIRECTIONS

① Take path immediately to R of Buck Inn (SP Windy Pike). On entering field head for its far RH corner, where you cross a small stream and, a few yards beyond, a stile on R. Cross next field diagonally R, aiming towards distant farm buildings, to locate footbridge. ② Climb R up far bank to wm, then straight across field to stile (wm). Continue forward alongside hawthorns to another stile. ③ Turn R alongside hedge, through gate and follow farm road. ④ Through next gate turn L (off farm road) and follow hedge on L. Turn R at field-corner to follow old, green, tree-lined track. Re-join farm road at a cattle-grid, and at tarmac lane keep straight on. ⑤ At T-junction turn L along road (Bolton by Bowland 2). ⑥ Turn L (FP sign) into farmyard. Immediately past three hoppers go R through wooden gate then L through metal gates and follow hedge on R down to stile in corner. ⑦ Straight on. At end of next field cross slab bridge and stile then turn L to cross, via stiles, a belt of trees and a farm track. ⑧ Straight across field to 'stile' (a short bit of wooden fence) then bear slightly R across big field to stile at far corner. ⑨ Maintain direction to far RH corner of next field. Cross stile and turn L to pass, via stiles, through small plantation. ⑩ Turn R to descend long field to stile near its LH corner. ⑪ Turn L along lane. Keep R at junction. ⑫ Cross bridge over Ribble and take track to L of buildings (BW sign). At top of hill keep R over cattle-grid then L (straight on). ⑬ Cross hospital drive to go down narrow tarmac lane. Cross bridge (Stock Beck) then fork sharp L up cart-track. ⑭ Turn L along main road. ⑮ At bend of road take gate/stile (BW sign) on L and climb to small gate to R of wooded knoll. Go forward through another gate and alongside fence on R to a broad path through woodland. ⑯ Turn L over Paythorne Bridge and follow road back up to Paythorne.

A large pack of hunting hounds is kennelled at Ellenthorpe.

(Map labels: PAYTHORNE, park here, ex-school, caravans, Bank Top, Hewitts Farm, barn, Paythorne Bridge, Loftrans Farm, fence, Loftrans Lane (track), Carters, Carter's Lane, farm road, reservoir, Nissen hut, O.S. column (funny place to find one), Monubent Head Farm, Close's Plantation, Fooden Moor, plastic trough, farm track, James's Plantation, Ellenthorpe (kennels), Walton Laithe, Gisburn Bridge, R. Ribble, Stock Beck, hospital, Gisburne Park, A 682, busy road, gatepost inscribed R 1903, MS (illustrated), tumulus, pond, Castle Haugh, R. Ribble)

Easy walking, but can be very muddy after rain. Mostly pathless pastures as far as point ⑪, then lanes and clear tracks. 1½ miles on motor-roads. No ladder-stiles, but at the time of writing (Feb 98) some of the fence-stiles presented a potential health hazard, being either on the point of collapse or decorated with exposed strands of barbed wire. This is lovely countryside – lush, peaceful and pastoral – and on a sunny autumn day the section between Gisburn Bridge and Stock Beck is an extravagant riot of colour.

PAYTHORNE

This ancient Domesday manor is best-known for its 'Salmon Sunday' – the Sunday nearest to November 20th – when Paythorne Bridge would be thronged with people hoping to witness the annual 'running' of salmon to their spawning beds higher upstream. In post-war years pollution of the lower Ribble, mainly from the rivers Calder and Darwen, caused a severe decline in the number of fish, but the pollution has now been reduced sufficiently to allow the salmon to run again more freely.

The Buck Inn is an ever-popular watering-hole, and the tiny Methodist chapel next door has served the community since 1830.

Paythorne Bridge – a medieval structure

GISBURNE PARK HALL IS GLORIOUSLY SITED ON AN EMINENCE OVERLOOKING THE CONFLUENCE OF STOCKS BECK AND THE RIBBLE. THE ELEGANT FAÇADE IS GEORGIAN, DATING FROM 1750, BUT THE HALL IS OLDER THAN THAT AND WAS ORIGINALLY CALLED LOWER HALL. THE IMMENSELY INFLUENTIAL LISTERS, WHOSE FAMILY SEAT THIS WAS, WERE LORDS OF RIBBLESDALE, WITH VAST ESTATES STRETCHING FROM CLITHEROE TO MALHAM. THE HALL IS NOW A PRIVATE HOSPITAL, AND ITS DRIVE PASSES THROUGH RICHLY WOODED PARKLAND WHERE WILD WHITE CATTLE USED TO ROAM. 'Gisburne' is the old spelling – the village dropped the 'e' about a century ago.

CASTLE HAUGH

This huge, wooded mound, encircled by a dry 7' ditch, is almost certainly the site of an early Norman motte and bailey castle. On top of the motte (hill) would have stood a wooden keep. The motte drops steeply to the river, and the bailey (fenced enclosure) would have been difficult to capture.

To Settle 10 Miles

Wild **MINK** may be seen along this stretch of the Ribble. Mink were introduced from the U.S.A. in 1929 as breeding stock for fur farms. Many escaped, and many more were deliberately released during the war, when there was no ready market for the pelts. Unlike most wild animals, the mink will kill even when not hungry, and can play havoc with fish stocks and breeding waterbirds.

16 THE RIBBLE GORGE 6¼ MILES

P Gisburn. At W end of village, by the Auction Mart. Parking space and toilets at junction of A59 and Mill Lane. Map ref: 826 487
It is also possible to park on the railway bridge 200yds along Mill Lane.

ROUTE DIRECTIONS

① Walk along Mill Lane.
② Turn L along Coppy House farm road. When it bends R go forward over cattle-grid. Pass L of house, and at bottom of yard turn R (RW sign) to kissing-gate. Bear R down field to kissing-gate and down to plank bridge. ③ Go R downstream for 60yds then bear L uphill. Pass to R of farm then R down farm road. ④ Before reaching house turn L (RW sign) to gate/stile. Follow fence forward, crossing to other side of it at a barn. ⑤ Cross tiny stream and turn R. Through gate/stile (wm) and turn L. Maintain level course, high above river, then follow RW signs to descend to fence-stile (wm) by river. Follow path downstream. ⑥ Pair of waymarks on L denote start of ALTERNATIVE ROUTE (see next page). For full walk follow riverside path for almost a mile. ⑦ After passing a patch of trees, and with a prominent limestone scar just ahead, turn L to climb away from river. Head for the more distant of two barns. Pass the near end of it, cross to stile in fence-angle and head for buildings. ⑧ Go through gate/stile (wm) to R of house and round buildings to stile. R along farm road for 60yds then L over stile (wm) and straight across field to stile. Descend field to gate (wm) at LH corner then forward along farm road to cross railway. ⑨ At farm road junction go L then R through gate by barn. Turn R and cross field to its far LH corner, then follow line of trees up to road. ⑩ L along road to stile on R. Bear L across field to double stile (wm). Head L to cross fence-stile (wm) and on to stile by short piece of wall. Head for building. ⑪ Pass R of building and on to next building. There's a wall-stile behind it. Cross field to gate to R of farm, then L along road. ⑫ Just past

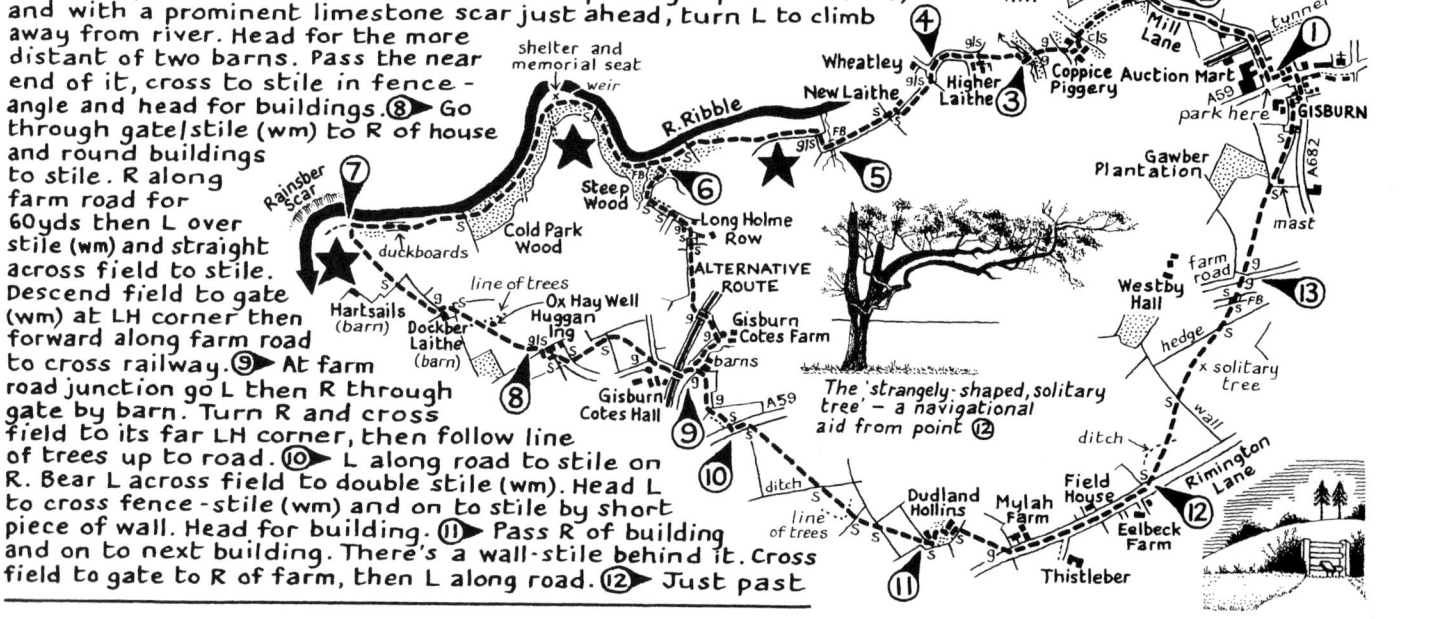

The 'strangely-shaped, solitary tree' – a navigational aid from point ⑫

42

Pathless pastures and 1¼ miles of glorious river scenery (*but see IMPORTANT NOTE below*). 3 ladder-stiles (2 with adjacent gates). ¾ mile on motor-roads. Dog-walkers will find some of the stiles a bit awkward. The riverside path through the gorge is by no means easy. Exposed roots present a hazard, and some inelegant scrambling is required to negotiate fallen trees. In wet weather the path is slippery; in very wet weather it's a ghastly quagmire.

IMPORTANT NOTE

THERE HAS BEEN A PROTRACTED AND BITTER DISPUTE OVER THE RIVERSIDE PATH, THE LOCAL LANDOWNER HAVING CONTESTED THE LEGITIMACY OF THE RIGHT-OF-WAY. AT THE TIME OF WRITING (Nov 98) THE MATTER WAS UNRESOLVED AND THE PATH WAS OPEN TO WALKERS. HOWEVER, IT SEEMS POSSIBLE – INDEED LIKELY – THAT THE RIGHT-OF-WAY WILL EVENTUALLY BE EXPUNGED AND RAMBLERS DENIED ACCESS TO THE FINEST STRETCH OF THE RIBBLE. I HAVE INCLUDED THE ROUTE IN THE HOPE THAT IT REMAINS OPEN. IF IT DOESN'T, YOU WILL HAVE TO USE THE ALTERNATIVE ROUTE FROM POINT 6 TO POINT 9. THE WALK WILL THEN BE 4¾ MILES.

ALTERNATIVE ROUTE Clear, waymarked path winds steeply up through trees, then runs along top edge of wooded ravine. Exit by stile (wm) and forward between fence and line of hawthorns. Forward to farm, and at first buildings take small gate on R. Cross ladder-stile, then another stile. Go straight ahead to cross railway bridge and on to farm. Turn R along farm road. At far side of second barn go L through gate at point ⑨.

(*main route cont.*) Eelbeck Farm take stile on L and head for strangely-shaped solitary tree. On passing it bear slightly R to stile (wm), then straight on to gate (wm). ⑬ Cross farm road and up big field to stile by mast. Forward with fence on R, then pass R of school and R down its drive. Go L to village centre and L again to Auction Mart.

GISBURN is a quaint and charming village. Peaceful, however, it is definitely not, for it is rent asunder by the constant stream of vehicles rumbling along the A59. Crossing the main street unscathed requires agility and a modicum of luck, and next-of-kin should be informed before an attempt is made. The beautiful church has a 13th C. porch and 14th C. tower, and its lovely stained glass includes medieval fragments. Gisburn has two splendid inns; until recently there were three, but the New Inn, by the entrance to Gisburne Park, is now extinct, as are the wild white cattle which once roamed the park and which gave the White Bull pub its name. An inscription on the porch of the Ribblesdale Arms informs us that it was built in 1635 and bears the name of Thomas Lister. The Listers were Lords of Ribblesdale and lived at Gisburne Park (a Georgian mansion now a private hospital).

● **GISBURN COTES HALL** displays a 1659 datestone above the porch. ● The railway was built by the LANCASHIRE and YORKSHIRE RAILWAY Co. and was completed in 1880.

RAINSBER SCAR, a limestone cliff at a bend of the river, is known as PUDSAY'S LEAP. In the 16th C. Sir William Pudsay made counterfeit money from silver obtained from his mine at Rimington. He was found out, and it is said that in fleeing from his pursuers he leapt his horse down the Scar. He escaped unhurt, and was later pardoned by Elizabeth I.

● ● ●

WESTBY HALL was, until the late 1700s the home of the Listers, and has connections with the so-called 'Pendle Witches'. In 1612 Jennet Preston was charged with 'causing the death, by charms and sorcery, of Thomas Lister, of Westby Hall'. Evidence was given that after Lister's death she was made to touch the corpse, which thereupon began to bleed'. She was tried at York Assizes, found guilty and hanged.

Wᵐ Rushworth
Field House
1819
Repeat no grievances but Study to be quiet and Mind your own business

TABLET IN THE WALL OF FIELD HOUSE

17 BEACON HILL
6½ MILES

ROUTE DIRECTIONS

① Walk along Bolton by Bowland road and over Sawley Bridge. ② At fork go L along Grindleton road. Turn R up to Friends' Meeting House and keep straight on, passing to immediate L of garage (looks private) to gate/stile. Straight on up through small plantation. ③ Make for stile well to R of house. Go forward with hedge on L, and when it turns away keep straight on past LH of two ash trees to descend to stile and footbridge. ④ Climb field to stile (wm), continue up LH side of fields, then bear R to house. ⑤ Take gate/stile to stone path through front garden. Cross stile into yard, then over cattle-grid to follow farm road through Till House Farm. At last farm building take stile (wm) up on R, then forward alongside fence to stile (wm). ⑥ Cross field to fence-stile, but don't use it. Turn L through wall-gateway and forward to stile. Bear slightly L in next field and head for farm. ⑦ Just before farm cross fence-stile. Through gates to pass L of farm. Follow wall on L, turning L with it into walled green lane. At its end turn L up road. ⑧ Take gate (FP sign) on R. Forward to stile, then up LH side of fenced gully. Keep on up with wall on R (detour L to visit O.S. column), then descend track between walls to plantation. ⑨ Turn L along path between trees and wall. It soon becomes a wide forest track. At wm turn R to follow path (wm) through forest to stile. ⑩ Turn L up road, then R through small gate (BW sign) and along clear green track to gate by narrow strip of woodland. ⑪ Track continues by wall, eventually developing into a farm road. ⑫ Turn L at T-junction to follow lane into Grindleton. ⑬ Just past bus terminus turn L (FP sign) up track, then R to follow Back Lane

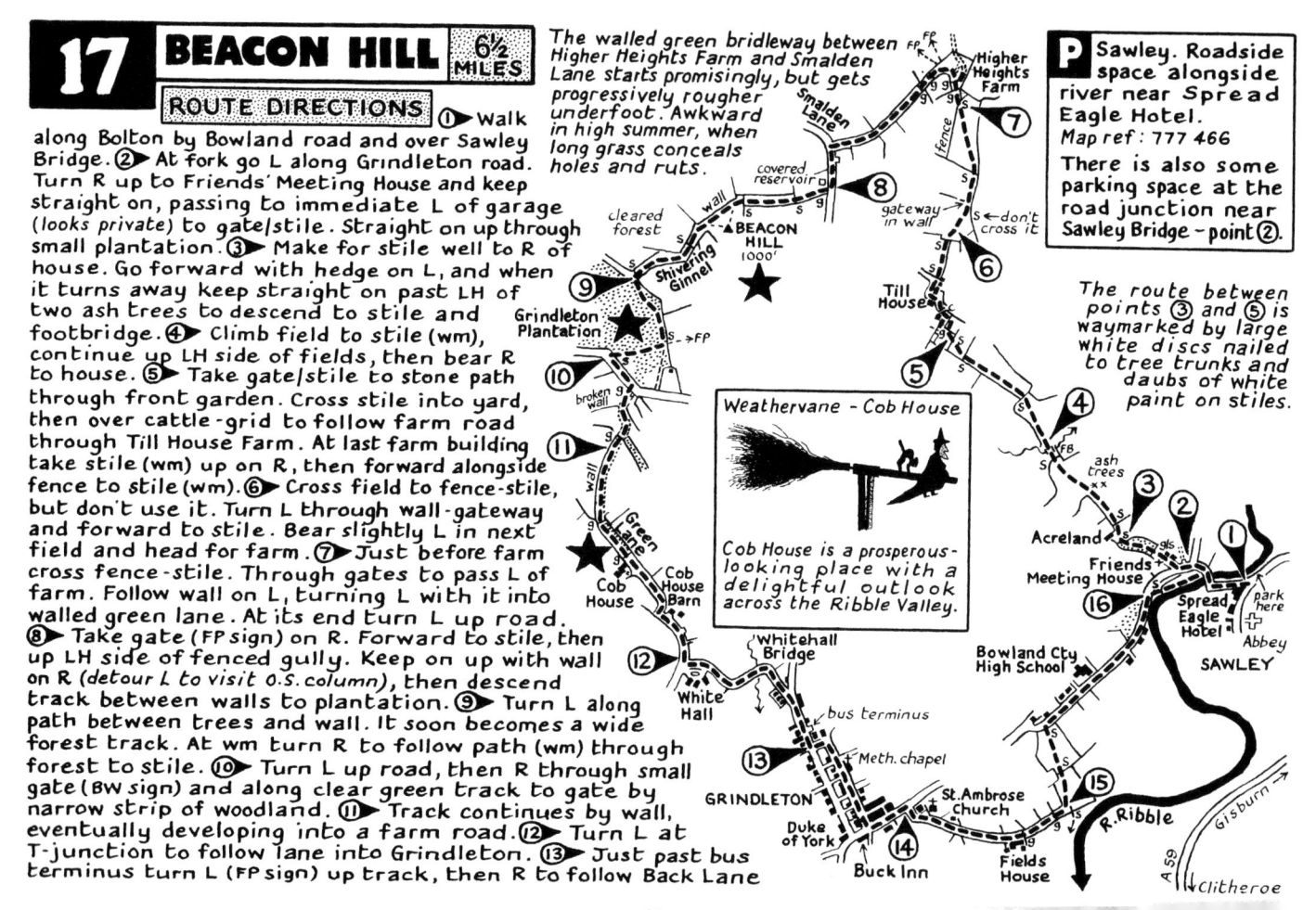

The walled green bridleway between Higher Heights Farm and Smalden Lane starts promisingly, but gets progressively rougher underfoot. Awkward in high summer, when long grass conceals holes and ruts.

Weathervane - Cob House

Cob House is a prosperous-looking place with a delightful outlook across the Ribble Valley.

P Sawley. Roadside space alongside river near Spread Eagle Hotel.
Map ref: 777 466
There is also some parking space at the road junction near Sawley Bridge – point ②.

The route between points ③ and ⑤ is waymarked by large white discs nailed to tree trunks and daubs of white paint on stiles.

Map labels: Higher Heights Farm; Smalden Lane; fence; covered reservoir; cleared forest; wall; gateway in wall; don't cross it; ⑧ ⑦ ⑥; BEACON HILL 1000'; Shivering Ginnel; Till House; Grindleton Plantation; ⑨; ⑤; ④; ash trees; FB; ③ ② ①; broken wall; ⑩; Acreland; Friends Meeting House; ⑪; ⑯; Spread Eagle Hotel; park here; Abbey; SAWLEY; Green Lane; Cob House; Cob House Barn; ⑫; Whitehall Bridge; White Hall; Bowland Cty High School; bus terminus; Meth. chapel; ⑬; GRINDLETON; Duke of York; ⑭; Buck Inn; St. Ambrose Church; Fields House; ⑮; R. Ribble; A59; Gisburn; Clitheroe

👣 Moderately strenuous. The outward half – from Sawley to the top of Beacon Hill – involves over 800' of uphill work, but it's very gradual, with no steep gradients. Route-finding easy, with plenty of waymarks. Varied terrain, including pathless pastures, green lanes and forest tracks. Less than a mile on motor-roads. Only 1 ladder-stile (and that's a diddy one). Beacon Hill is one of the finest viewpoints in the Ribble Valley.

down to main road. Turn L. ⑭➤ Turn R at C.E. School. Follow lane to pass L of farm and along green lane between hedges. ⑮➤ At end of enclosed section turn L (RW sign) to climb two fields. Turn R along road. ⑯➤ Go R over stile (FP sign) and along riverbank to Sawley Bridge. Turn R along road.

Forest of Bowland

Above Sawley and Grindleton the gentle slopes of the Ribble Valley merge into the verdant south-eastern foothills of the magnificent Forest of Bowland, the most extensive tract of unspoiled countryside in Lancashire. Featured on the sign is the hen harrier, a rare bird of prey which breeds in a few of Bowland's wildest and remotest localities.

SAWLEY

Spread Eagle Hotel

An attractive village with several interesting buildings, Sawley is best-known for its Cistercian abbey ruins.

SOME FACTS ABOUT SALLEY ABBEY

● Founded 1147 ● Ruins reveal a lack of wealth - built with a mixture of black shale and boulder stones ● Struggled to compete with a rival abbey founded at Whalley in 1296 ● Housed only 21 monks when dissolved by Henry VIII in 1536 ● William Trafford, the last abbot, was executed 10th March 1537 for his involvement in the Pilgrimage of Grace (a rebellion to re-establish the monastic way of life) ● The arch over a nearby field gateway has no connection with the abbey; it was built in the 1840s.

BEACON HILL is of modest height, but the view from its O.S. column (S 5159) is quite remarkable. To the SE dear old Pendle smiles or frowns (depending on the weather) at us across the lush Ribble Valley. The northern aspect presents a sweeping panorama from the dark fells of Bowland around to the shapely peaks of the Yorkshire Dales, with Ingleborough and Penyghent highly prominent.

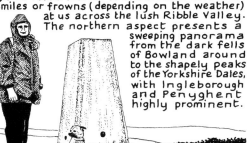

lych-gate, Parish Church of St. Ambrose, Grindleton

GRINDLETON, ancient enough to appear in the Domesday Book, takes its name from the bygone local industry of quarrying and the manufacture of grindstones. It is a place of numerous alleyways and ginnels, and many of the houses are old handloom-weavers' cottages. In the 17th C. one Rodger Brierly, Minister of the Gospel at Grindleton and a 'faithful and pious Servant of Jesus Christ', founded a religious sect here which became known as 'Grindletonians'. He was much persecuted, at one time being imprisoned at York facing 50 charges of false teaching.

18 PENDLE HILL — 6 MILES

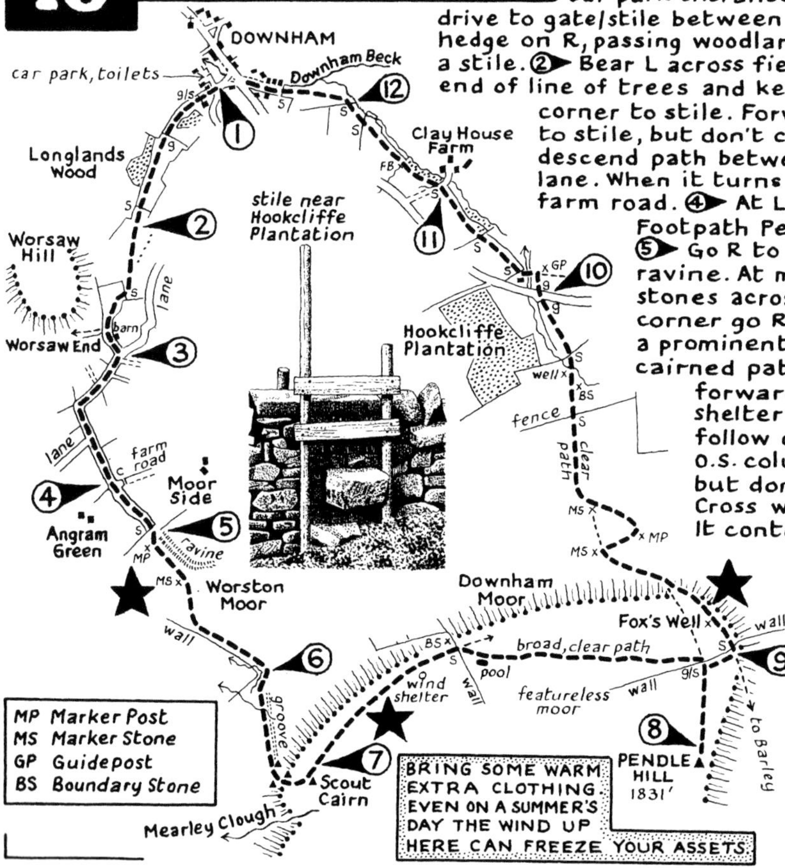

ROUTE DIRECTIONS

① From car park entrance go R (FP sign) up drive to gate/stile between two houses. Follow hedge on R, passing woodland on R to reach a stile. ② Bear L across field, passing far end of line of trees and keeping L of fence-corner to stile. Forward to R of hedge to stile, but don't cross it. Instead descend path between hedges, passing a barn. ③ Turn R along lane. When it turns R keep straight on (SP Cul-de-sac) up tarmac farm road. ④ At L bend of farm road go straight on (Concessionary Footpath Pendle Hill) up green path to stile at its end. ⑤ Go R to marker-post then climb steeply alongside ravine. At marker-stone bear R and follow more marker-stones across moor to wall. Climb alongside it. ⑥ At wall-corner go R towards marker-stone, then climb alongside a prominent groove slanting up hillside. Eventually a cairned path swings L up to large memorial cairn. ⑦ Go forward with escarpment on your L, passing a wind shelter to reach ladder-stile in crosswall. Bear R to follow clear path to gate/ladder-stile, then climb to O.S. column at summit. ⑧ Return to gate/ladder-stile but don't cross. Turn R and follow wall for 80 yds. ⑨ Cross wall at stone stile to path leading directly away. It contours hillside before dropping to a marker-stone. Follow markers to zig-zag down to a clear path passing to R of plantation. ⑩ Cross road to swing-gate (FP Downham), drop to guidepost and turn L. At barn take stile (wm) on R and descend RH side of fields. ⑪ Cross farm road to wall-stile (wm) and again descend RH side of fields. ⑫ From stile (wm) by a tree-stump go ½ L across the field, aiming towards a cluster of house chimneys. Walk alongside a stream to reach a stile into a lane at the bottom of the village. Feed the ducks and walk round Downham to expend any surplus energy.

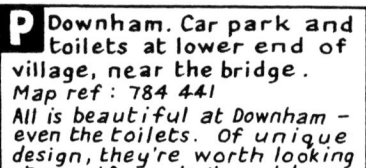

P Downham. Car park and toilets at lower end of village, near the bridge.
Map ref: 784 441
All is beautiful at Downham – even the toilets. Of unique design, they're worth looking at even if you don't want to go.

Map labels
DOWNHAM
car park, toilets
Downham Beck
Longlands Wood
Clay House Farm
Worsaw Hill
stile near Hookcliffe Plantation
Hookcliffe Plantation
Worsaw End
barn
lane
farm road
Moor Side
Angram Green
ravine
Worston Moor
wall
Downham Moor
Fox's Well
broad, clear path
pool
wind shelter
featureless moor
groove
Scout Cairn
Mearley Clough
PENDLE HILL 1831'
to Barley
fence
clear path
well
MP Marker Post
MS Marker Stone
GP Guidepost
BS Boundary Stone

BRING SOME WARM EXTRA CLOTHING EVEN ON A SUMMER'S DAY THE WIND UP HERE CAN FREEZE YOUR ASSETS

18

Generally easy walking, but with one strenuous section between points ⑤ and ⑦. This entails a climb - steep in places - of over 1000'. The low-level routes to and from the hill are through pathless pastures. On the hill the paths are mostly well-defined, with plenty of waymarks, but DON'T GO WITHOUT A COMPASS - mist can descend suddenly on Pendle. 2 ladder-stiles (1 with adjacent gate - which is a fat lot of use 'cos it's padlocked). Motor-road walking negligible. A great walk with exceptional views.

DOWNHAM

NEC ARROGO NEC DUBITO

DOWNHAM is undeniably the loveliest village in the Ribble Valley, if not in the whole of Lancashire. Proudly and lovingly maintained, it has won many awards for its beauty and, despite being overrun by tourists and trippers, remains remarkably unspoiled and uncommercialised. DOWNHAM HALL, at the N end of the village, has been the family seat of the ASSHETONS (armorial shield and motto shown left) since 1558. This Elizabethan mansion was extensively rebuilt in Georgian style in 1835. ST. LEONARD'S CHURCH was built as recently as 1910, though the tower has survived from a 15th C. church which was demolished in 1800. The late Queen Mary regarded the view from the porch as the most beautiful from any church porch in the land. At the lower end of the village, near the bridge, stands OLD WELL HALL, a superb Tudor house, and there are clusters of 18th. and 19th.C. HANDLOOM WEAVERS' COTTAGES. Children love to splash around in the pebbly stream, and corpulent mallard are equally happy gorging themselves on a never-ending supply of visitors' titbits. The highly-acclaimed film 'WHISTLE DOWN THE WIND', starring Hayley Mills, was shot on location in the village and at Worsaw End in 1961.

Downham

PENDLE HILL dominates the surrounding countryside to a greater extent than does, perhaps, any other hill in the land. It is not a great mountain; in fact it is not a mountain at all, its summit failing by 169' to achieve that distinction. However, because of its isolated position - between the main South Pennine Chain and the Bowland Fells - it rises majestically and appears much higher than it really is. What Pendle lacks in height it certainly makes up for in girth, being no less than seven miles long and covering an area of some twenty-five square miles. The top of the hill is a vast plateau of peat hags and coarse grasses, and the view must be one of the finest in England - a magnificent panorama of infinite variety and charm. Legends of witchcraft and black magic, strange superstitions and whispered tales of supernatural happenings have given Pendle an almost mystical atmosphere. Pass close to the hill on a wild, drab winter's day and you half-expect to see a besom-mounted witch gliding silently by.

SCOUT CAIRN is a prominent Ribble Valley landmark, and 3 memorial tablets built into the splendidly constructed 10' monument explain its name. All the hard work is now behind you, and the walk from the cairn to the crosswall, along the rim of Pendle's northern escarpment, is the finest section of the route.

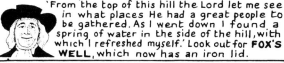

GEORGE FOX, founder of the Quakers, climbed Pendle in 1652, found inspiration there and afterwards wrote, 'From the top of this hill the Lord let me see in what places He had a great people to be gathered. As I went down I found a spring of water in the side of the hill, with which I refreshed myself.' Look out for **FOX'S WELL**, which now has an iron lid.

For more - MUCH more - about PENDLE and the WITCHES, rush out NOW and buy WALKS IN LANCASHIRE WITCH COUNTRY (See P.4)

19 WEST BRADFORD FELL 7¾ MILES

ROUTE DIRECTIONS

① Cross bridge and follow road. At LH bend cross stile (FP sign) to footbridges and riverside path. ② Turn L up to stile (wm) and along fenced path. Turn L along road. ③ Turn R (BW Waddington Fell) up tarmac lane. Beyond Greenbanks continue uphill on stony track. ④ Turn L through gate immediately to L of cattle-grid and farm road. Go slightly L across field, over two fence-stiles, then aim just to R of farm beyond trees to drop to gate in wall. ⑤ Cross footbridge and climb to farm. Follow cart-track to pass through farmyard and straight on along farm road. ⑥ At T-junction turn R up tarmac lane. When it bends L go straight on through gate to cart-track. ⑦ Turn R over high ladder-stile (wm) and L up field to wall-stile (wm) by old iron notice. Bear R to pass wall-corner, then cross rushy field (pile of stones and plank bridge mid-way) to its far corner. Cross broken wall and forward (wm) with wall on L. Turn L through gate and along walled track. ⑧ Go L up road alongside plantation. ⑨ Turn L through scanty ruins (St. Clares), then R through gap in wall to follow old cart-track swinging L towards ruined farm. Through gate and up alongside ditch on L, turning L at top to ruin. ⑩ Through gate and turn R up thin path in heather by wall. At its end turn L down walled track. Keep straight on down past a barn to join a tarmac lane. ⑪ Turn L (FP sign) at house and follow waymarks through farmyard. In field bear R over stile and head for next farm. ⑫ Turn L to pass L of house and down rough track to ford. Follow track downstream, ignoring big ladder-stile on R. Go through gate/stile and immediately R over stile. Cross diagonally L to stile, then down

P Bradford Bridge, just south of West Bradford. Parking space (4-5 cars) at S end of bridge. Map ref: 745 439

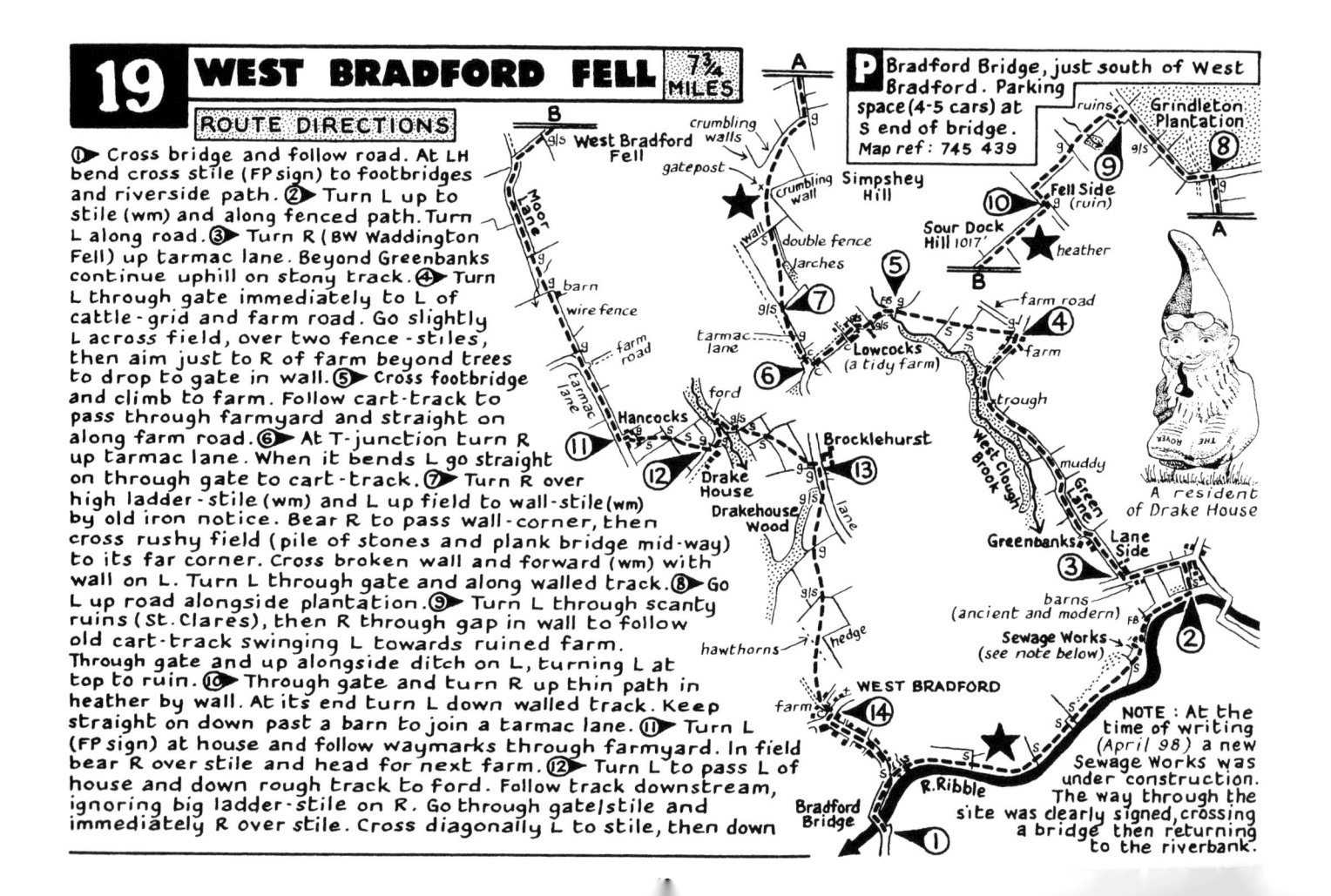

A resident of Drake House

NOTE: At the time of writing (April 98) a new Sewage Works was under construction. The way through the site was clearly signed, crossing a bridge then returning to the riverbank.

19

A longish walk (by J. Keighley standards), and moderately strenuous, though with no steep gradients. The terrain is very varied, and includes riverside paths, tarmac lanes, farm roads, pathless pastures and windswept heather moorland. 3 ladder-stiles (2 with adjacent gates). ¾ mile on motor-roads.

THIS SPLENDID WALK OFFERS THE MOST MARVELLOUS VIEWS OF PENDLE, BUT UNFORTUNATELY ONE CANNOT LOOK TOWARDS THIS NOBLE HILL WITHOUT THE EYE BEING ASSAILED BY THE MOST HIDEOUS EYESORE IN RURAL LANCASHIRE, VIZ, THE RIBBLE CEMENT WORKS. POLLUTING THE SKY WITH SMOKE AND THE LAND WITH DUST, THIS MONSTROUS ENVIRONMENTAL DISASTER LOOMS MALEVOLENTLY OVER CLITHEROE, COMPLETELY SPOILING AN OTHERWISE ENTIRELY CHARMING LITTLE TOWN AND CAUSING ITS INHABITANTS TO WONDER IF THEIR HEALTH IS BEING DAMAGED.

to gates to R of farm. ⑬► R along lane. In 120 yds take gate/stile on R and cross field, keeping roughly parallel with wood, to gate in fence. Aim slightly to R of cement works to locate gate/stile, then bear slightly R to pass hedge-corner. Maintain direction to pass through farmyard. ⑭► R along road. In a few yards turn L (Clitheroe 2) and follow road back to Bradford Bridge.

The Hippings House

WEST BRADFORD

IS A PLEASANT LITTLE VILLAGE WHICH HAS ENJOYED A LONG AND LARGELY UNEVENTFUL HISTORY. THE NAME 'BRADFORD' IS A DERIVATION OF 'BROADFORD' — A WIDE, SHALLOW CROSSING PLACE (OF THE RIBBLE). THE COTTAGE ILLUSTRATED, WHICH IS PASSED ALMOST AT THE END OF THE WALK, IS A TYPICAL EXAMPLE OF WEST BRADFORD'S MANY ATTRACTIVE AND WELL-KEPT HOUSES, SOME OF WHICH ARE ACCESSED BY QUAINT LITTLE STONE BRIDGES SPANNING A TINY CHUCKLING STREAM. IN RECENT YEARS, HOWEVER, WEST BRADFORD HAS GROWN CONSIDERABLY DUE TO EXTENSIVE RESIDENTIAL DEVELOPMENT, AND THE MODERN 'COMMUTER HOUSING' HAS TO SOME EXTENT ALTERED THE CHARACTER OF THE VILLAGE. THE OLD COTTON MILL HAS BEEN CONVERTED INTO HOUSES AND APARTMENTS. IN SEPTEMBER 1931 WEST BRADFORD HAD A FLEETING MOMENT OF UNACCUSTOMED NATIONAL PROMINENCE WHEN MAHATMA GANDHI STAYED AT HEYS FARM. THE ILLUSTRIOUS INDIAN STATESMAN WAS ON A FACT-FINDING TOUR OF LANCASHIRE'S COTTON MILLS.

GANDHI (born 1869) led the struggle for Indian independence and was jailed many times for his non-violent campaigns against British rule. He was assassinated on 30 January 1948 on his way to a prayer meeting.

Fell Side – deserted, lonely and desolate

Drake House

Riverside path

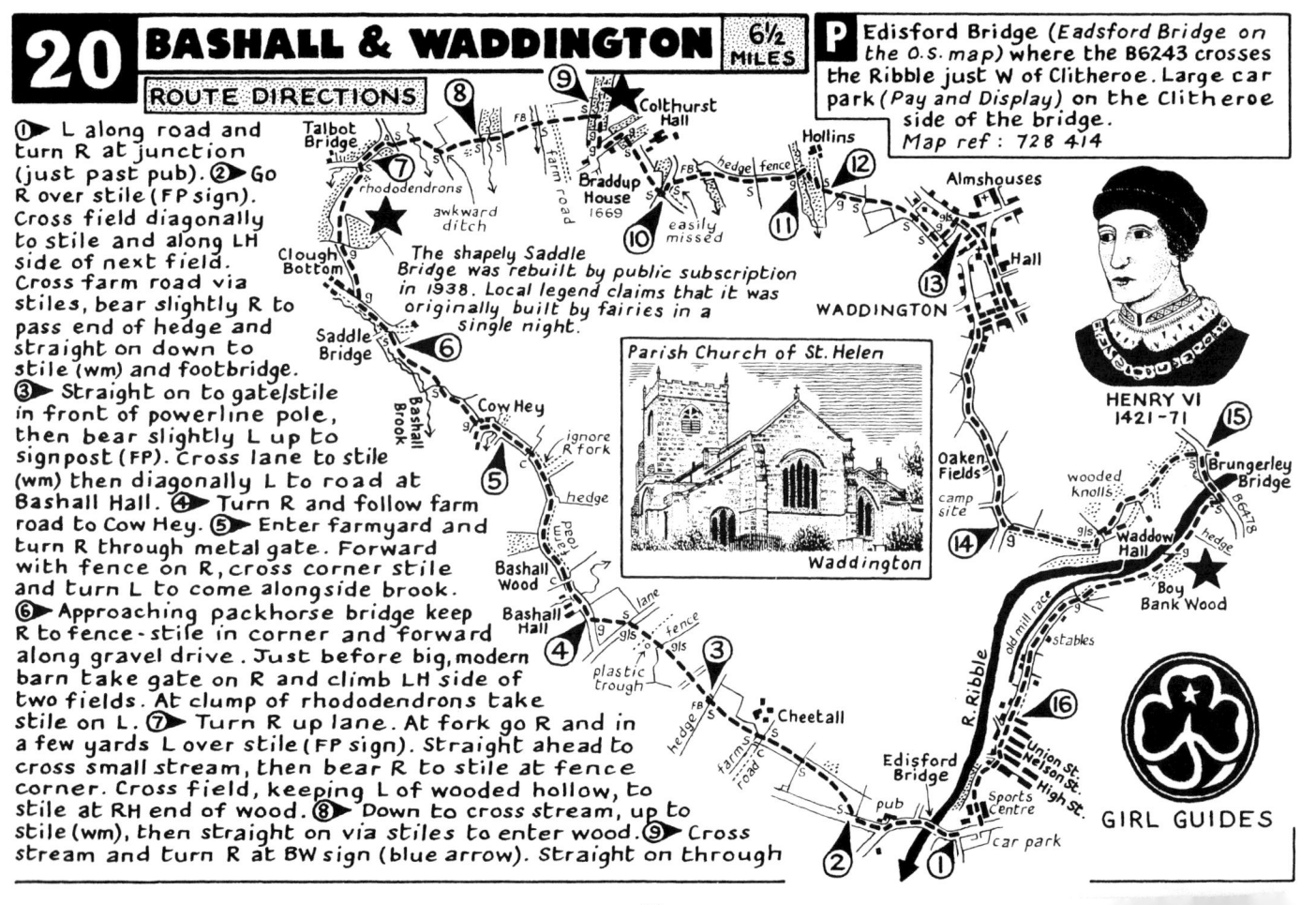

20 BASHALL & WADDINGTON

6½ MILES

ROUTE DIRECTIONS

P Edisford Bridge (*Eadsford Bridge on the O.S. map*) where the B6243 crosses the Ribble just W of Clitheroe. Large car park (*Pay and Display*) on the Clitheroe side of the bridge. Map ref: 728 414

①▶ L along road and turn R at junction (just past pub). **②▶** Go R over stile (FP sign). Cross field diagonally to stile and along LH side of next field. Cross farm road via stiles, bear slightly R to pass end of hedge and straight on down to stile (wm) and footbridge. **③▶** Straight on to gate/stile in front of powerline pole, then bear slightly L up to signpost (FP). Cross lane to stile (wm) then diagonally L to road at Bashall Hall. **④▶** Turn R and follow farm road to Cow Hey. **⑤▶** Enter farmyard and turn R through metal gate. Forward with fence on R, cross corner stile and turn L to come alongside brook. **⑥▶** Approaching packhorse bridge keep R to fence-stile in corner and forward along gravel drive. Just before big, modern barn take gate on R and climb LH side of two fields. At clump of rhododendrons take stile on L. **⑦▶** Turn R up lane. At fork go R and in a few yards L over stile (FP sign). Straight ahead to cross small stream, then bear R to stile at fence corner. Cross field, keeping L of wooded hollow, to stile at RH end of wood. **⑧▶** Down to cross stream, up to stile (wm), then straight on via stiles to enter wood. **⑨▶** Cross stream and turn R at BW sign (blue arrow). Straight on through

The shapely Saddle Bridge was rebuilt by public subscription in 1938. Local legend claims that it was originally built by fairies in a single night.

Parish Church of St. Helen

Waddington

HENRY VI
1421-71

GIRL GUIDES

Very easy walking, but pay careful attention to Route Directions. The first part of the walk, as far as Waddington, is rather complex, with few visible paths and some none-too-obvious stiles. No ladder-stiles. 1¼ miles on motor-roads.

wood and down to road. Turn L and at FP sign go R through swing-gate. Pass through trees and along LH side of field to stile. ⑩▶ L up farm road, in a few yards taking stile on R. Straight ahead past single ash tree to footbridge. Go up to field boundary and follow it to R. ⑪▶ Through gate and up cart-track. When it swings L go R alongside hedge to locate stile. ⑫▶ Forward through gate and follow hedge on L to stile. Straight on, towards distant works chimney. At wall fork R down to stile and along enclosed path. Cross slab bridge to gate on L and cross field to Waddington. ⑬▶ Turn R and go straight down main street, turn R along Waddow View and L at T-junction. ⑭▶ L through gate (FP sign) and along cart-track. At gate (Keep Out) turn L (FP sign) up to gate/stile. Forward alongside wall, then L (FP sign) along tarmac drive. Follow FP signs. ⑮▶ Turn R down road, cross bridge and R over stile to riverside path. Through patch of woodland, ignoring steps on L, then bear L up to swing-gate. Follow cart-track. ⑯▶ Straight on, passing end of Union St. and Nelson St. Just around a LH bend (High St.) turn R up into playing-fields. Go R around field and between big Sports Centre buildings to road and car park.

BASHALL HALL

It was from this ancient house that the Talbots and their men sallied forth in 1464 to capture Henry VI. The Hall, which was restored in the 1970s, is a miscellany of architectural styles ranging from Elizabethan to Georgian. The timbered building near the bridge was once a barracks, with troops occupying the upper storey and horses stabled below.

WADDOW HALL

set in lovely grounds sloping down to the Ribble, was built by the Tempests but passed out of their hands in 1657 when the boozing and gambling of Richard Tempest ruined the estate. It has been owned by the Girl Guides Association since 1928, and is now used as a Commonwealth Training Centre.

font, Waddington Church

WADDINGTON

In the author's opinion the Ribble Valley's third prettiest village — after Downham and Bolton-by-Bowland. Detour L at the Higher Buck Inn to see the 18th.C.almshouses known as 'The Widows' Hospital'. The church is dedicated to St.Helen (c 248-328), mother of Constantine the Great, the first Christian emperor of Rome. Depicted in stained glass are St.Helen, King Henry VI and Wada, a Saxon chieftain after whom the village is named. There is a medieval font, and the benches in the Browsholme Chapel are late-Stuart. Near the church are an old pinfold (pound for stray animals) and the village stocks. Undoubtedly the village's most eye-catching feature is the beautiful Garden of Remembrance, with its chuckling stream, tiny bridge, sundial and floral displays. Waddington Hall, unfortunately, cannot be well-seen, being obscured by trees and a high wall.

FOR NOTES ON EDISFORD BRIDGE SEE WALK 21

BRUNGERLEY

During the troubled times of the Wars of the Roses the Lancastrian King Henry VI found refuge at Waddington Hall. However, his presence there was discovered by the Yorkists, and in attempting to flee he was captured at Brungerley stepping-stones (there was no bridge then). It is said that he was made to ride to London sitting back-to-front on his horse. A flimsy bridge built in 1801 was soon destroyed by floods, and was replaced by the present bridge in 1816.

21 GREAT MITTON — 5¾ MILES

ROUTE DIRECTIONS

P Edisford Bridge (*Eadsford Bridge* on the O.S. map) where the B6243 crosses the Ribble just W of Clitheroe. Large car park (Pay and Display) on the Clitheroe side of the bridge.
Map ref: 728 414

① Walk down roadside path and turn L past café to follow riverside path. **②** Through swing-gate (wm RW) to clear path rising through bushes. Through another gate and go L diagonally across field to gate. **③** Turn R then L (RW sign) down lane. Turn R along road. **④** Keep R (straight on) into farmyard. Keep R (wm) of all farm buildings, then along farm track to riverside path. **⑤** At weir bear slightly L. Cross footbridge and rise to gate (wm). **⑥** Follow RH field boundary. Cross stile at fence angle and again keep alongside RH field boundary. Pass L of buildings to gate. **⑦** Turn R along road. At junction keep straight on (but detour R along Church Lane to visit church). **⑧** Go L (Hurst Green and Longridge) at next junction. **⑨** Just before cottages turn R (FP sign) over stile in hedge (to view Lower Hodder bridges continue a little further along road, then return). Walk up alongside edge of wood. Pass, via stiles, through a narrow arm of the wood, then continue forward alongside the trees. **⑩** When the wood turns away L keep straight on, passing to L of solitary tree. Cross the big field to gate/stile at its far LH corner. **⑪** Turn L and cross road-junction to fence-stile (FP sign). Forward across field and pass R of copse to stile in corner. **⑫** Straight on, heading towards centre of wood. Go through gate/stile in wall on L, then keep L of bank to follow it round to farm track. Turn R along track down to gate in corner. **⑬** Forward with wall on L, through gate/stile and follow hedge on R to next field-corner. **⑭** Turn R over fence-stile and follow hedge on L. Go L over fence-stile (just beyond a gate) and forward across big field, aiming towards 2 distant spires and Clitheroe Castle. Cross fence-stile and on to double-stile-cum-footbridge in hedge. Follow RH field boundary to wall-stile. **⑮** Go L across field to gate. Turn R along road and L at junction.

The rich farmland here is an ideal habitat for rooks.

21

Easy walking, mostly through pastures and meadows, but with 1½ miles on motor-roads. Some fine river scenery. No ladder-stiles. It would be best not to do this walk in early- or mid-summer, when long (and possibly very wet) grass will impede progress, and damage may be caused to hay crops. ALWAYS WALK IN SINGLE FILE ACROSS MEADOWLAND.

Eadsford

In 1137 a fearful battle was waged here at the ford (there was no bridge in those days) when local Norman forces came into conflict with a marauding Scots army. The result was an away win, and legend tells us that so ferocious was the combat that the river 'ran with blood.' It is known that a wooden bridge had been built by 1339, and this was replaced by a medieval stone structure, the ribwork of which is still visible under the central arch. Edisford is a recreational area now, and a splendid one too, boasting a swimming pool and leisure centre, children's playground, caravan/camping site, miniature railway, cafe and toilets.

Pied Wagtail

THE RIVERSIDE PATH, taking us downstream from the bridge along a lovely stretch of the Ribble, is lined with hawthorn and willow, and in spring and summer there are wild flowers in profusion to delight the eye. The river attracts a rich variety of birdlife — sand martins, swallows, dippers, wagtails and exceptionally tame and well-fed ducks.

Stones above the doorway of the Three Fishes — thought to be from Whalley Abbey.

GREAT MITTON, though but a tiny hamlet, has several buildings of note. The 15th C LOWER MITTON HALL (to the L at point ⑦) is now a restaurant. The OLD HALL (by the church) pre-dates it by a century. Its fine mullioned windows are best seen from the vicinity of the Aspinall Arms. Building of the superb little CHURCH began during the reign of Henry III (1216-72) and the tower was added in 1438. The floor of the nave slopes down to a priceless Elizabethan screen. The Shireburn Chapel was built in 1440 and rebuilt 1594. Though somewhat at odds with the general architecture of the church, it is lovely in its own right and contains some splendid tombs of this great local family.

The Aspinall Arms takes its name from a prominent local family.

THE GRACEFUL ARCHES OF THE OLD **LOWER HODDER BRIDGE** HAVE SPANNED THE HODDER SINCE 1562. CROMWELL IS SAID TO HAVE MARCHED HIS TROOPS OVER IT EN ROUTE FOR THE BATTLE OF PRESTON IN 1648, BUT THIS IS MOST UNLIKELY. IT IS, HOWEVER, KNOWN LOCALLY AS CROMWELL'S BRIDGE. THE NEW BRIDGE WAS BUILT BY JOHN MACADAM IN 1826.

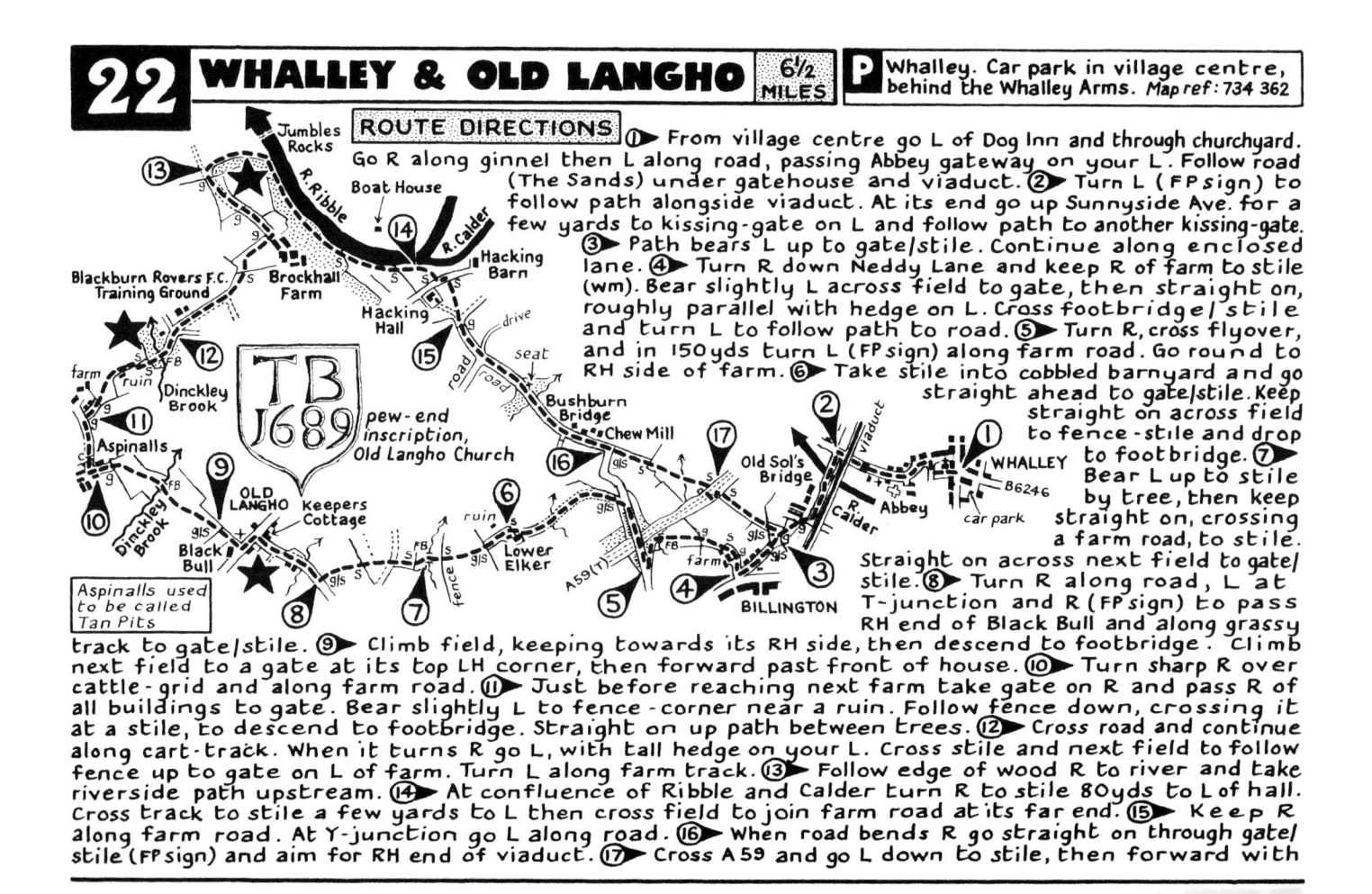

22 WHALLEY & OLD LANGHO

6½ MILES

P Whalley. Car park in village centre, behind the Whalley Arms. Map ref: 734 362

ROUTE DIRECTIONS

① From village centre go L of Dog Inn and through churchyard. Go R along ginnel then L along road, passing Abbey gateway on your L. Follow road (The Sands) under gatehouse and viaduct. ② Turn L (FP sign) to follow path alongside viaduct. At its end go up Sunnyside Ave. for a few yards to kissing-gate on L and follow path to another kissing-gate. ③ Path bears L up to gate/stile. Continue along enclosed lane. ④ Turn R down Neddy Lane and keep R of farm to stile (wm). Bear slightly L across field to gate, then straight on, roughly parallel with hedge on L. Cross footbridge/stile and turn L to follow path to road. ⑤ Turn R, cross flyover, and in 150yds turn L (FP sign) along farm road. Go round to RH side of farm. ⑥ Take stile into cobbled barnyard and go straight ahead to gate/stile. Keep straight on across field to fence-stile and drop to footbridge. ⑦ Bear L up to stile by tree, then keep straight on, crossing a farm road, to stile. Straight on across next field to gate/stile. ⑧ Turn R along road, L at T-junction and R (FP sign) to pass RH end of Black Bull and along grassy track to gate/stile. ⑨ Climb field, keeping towards its RH side, then descend to footbridge. Climb next field to a gate at its top LH corner, then forward past front of house. ⑩ Turn sharp R over cattle-grid and along farm road. ⑪ Just before reaching next farm take gate on R and pass R of all buildings to gate. Bear slightly L to fence-corner near a ruin. Follow fence down, crossing it at a stile, to descend to footbridge. Straight on up path between trees. ⑫ Cross road and continue along cart-track. When it turns R go L, with tall hedge on your L. Cross stile and next field to follow fence up to gate on L of farm. Turn L along farm track. ⑬ Follow edge of wood R to river and take riverside path upstream. ⑭ At confluence of Ribble and Calder turn R to stile 80yds to L of hall. Cross track to stile a few yards to L then cross field to join farm road at its far end. ⑮ Keep R along farm road. At Y-junction go L along road. ⑯ When road bends R go straight on through gate/stile (FP sign) and aim for RH end of viaduct. ⑰ Cross A59 and go L down to stile, then forward with

Map labels

Jumbles Rocks
R. Ribble
Boat House
R. Calder
Hacking Barn
Blackburn Rovers F.C. Training Ground
Brockhall Farm
Hacking Hall
drive
seat
road
TB J689 pew-end inscription, Old Langho Church
farm ruin
Dinckley Brook
Aspinalls
Dinckley Brook
OLD LANGHO Keepers Cottage
Black Bull
Aspinalls used to be called Tan Pits
Bushburn Bridge
Chew Mill
Lower Elker
fence
ruin
A59(T)
farm
BILLINGTON
Old Sol's Bridge
viaduct
R. Calder
Abbey
car park
WHALLEY
B6246

22

Generally very easy walking, but take care not to trip over hidden roots or fall through rotting plank bridges on the somewhat overgrown and slippery riverside path. Route-finding a bit complex, so please concentrate. No ladder-stiles. 1¼ miles on motor roads. Allow plenty of time if you intend to visit the abbey and the two churches.

fence on R. Pass small brick building to re-join outward route at kissing-gate.

WHALLEY

Twinned with VIHIERS FRANCE

This large village has sufficient charm and historical interest to attract thousands of visitors a year. THE SQUARE is the original village centre, and most of its buildings date from the 17th C., but in addition to these Whalley has many lovely old cottages and fine Tudor and Georgian houses. But Whalley's pride and joy is undoubtedly THE PARISH CHURCH OF ST. MARY AND ALL SAINTS — once the Mother Church for half of Lancashire. An excellent guidebook is available, and its pages are crammed with information on the wealth of treasures to be seen in and around a truly outstanding church with a history spanning 13 centuries. Building of the ABBEY began in 1308 and went on for 127 years. It became one of the most powerful Cistercian houses in the North of England. There are two fine gateways; the West Gate is backed rather incongruously by the red-brick railway VIADUCT built in 1850 and known as Whalley Arches. The metal bridge by which we cross the Calder is called OLD SOL'S BRIDGE. A plaque at its S. end tells you why.

THE HACKING FERRY Until 1954 a ferry operated across the Ribble near its confluence with the Calder. The old boatman's house still remains. An old ferry boat, found in a barn in 1983, can be seen in Clitheroe Castle Museum.

The Ostrich (struthio camelus) — not a common bird in the Ribble Valley

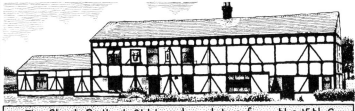

The Black Bull, at Old Langho, dates from the 15th C.

A bloody battle was fought at **BILLINGTON** in AD 798. The place was then called 'Billingahoh', and the name **LANGHO** is a shortened version of this ancient spelling. The **CHURCH OF ST. LEONARD** was built in 1557, reputedly with stone from the dismantled Whalley Abbey, and extensively restored in 1879. The pew ends bear the initials of their 'owners', with 17th C. dates. Sadly, this lovely little church was declared 'pastorally redundant' in 1990, and is now in the care of the Redundant Churches Fund. Should the door be locked when you call, the key may be obtained from the Black Bull, a few yards along the road.

Keepers Cottage, Old Langho

CHEW MILL, now converted, produced bobbins and clog soles until 1911.

HACKING HALL IS A NOBLE JACOBEAN MANSION BUILT IN 1607. ON THE AUTHOR'S LAST VISIT (May 98) A PAIR OF MALEVOLENT-LOOKING OSTRICHES WERE STRUTTING AROUND THE WALLED YARD IN FRONT OF THE HOUSE. NEARBY IS A MASSIVE TITHE BARN OF MONASTIC ORIGIN.

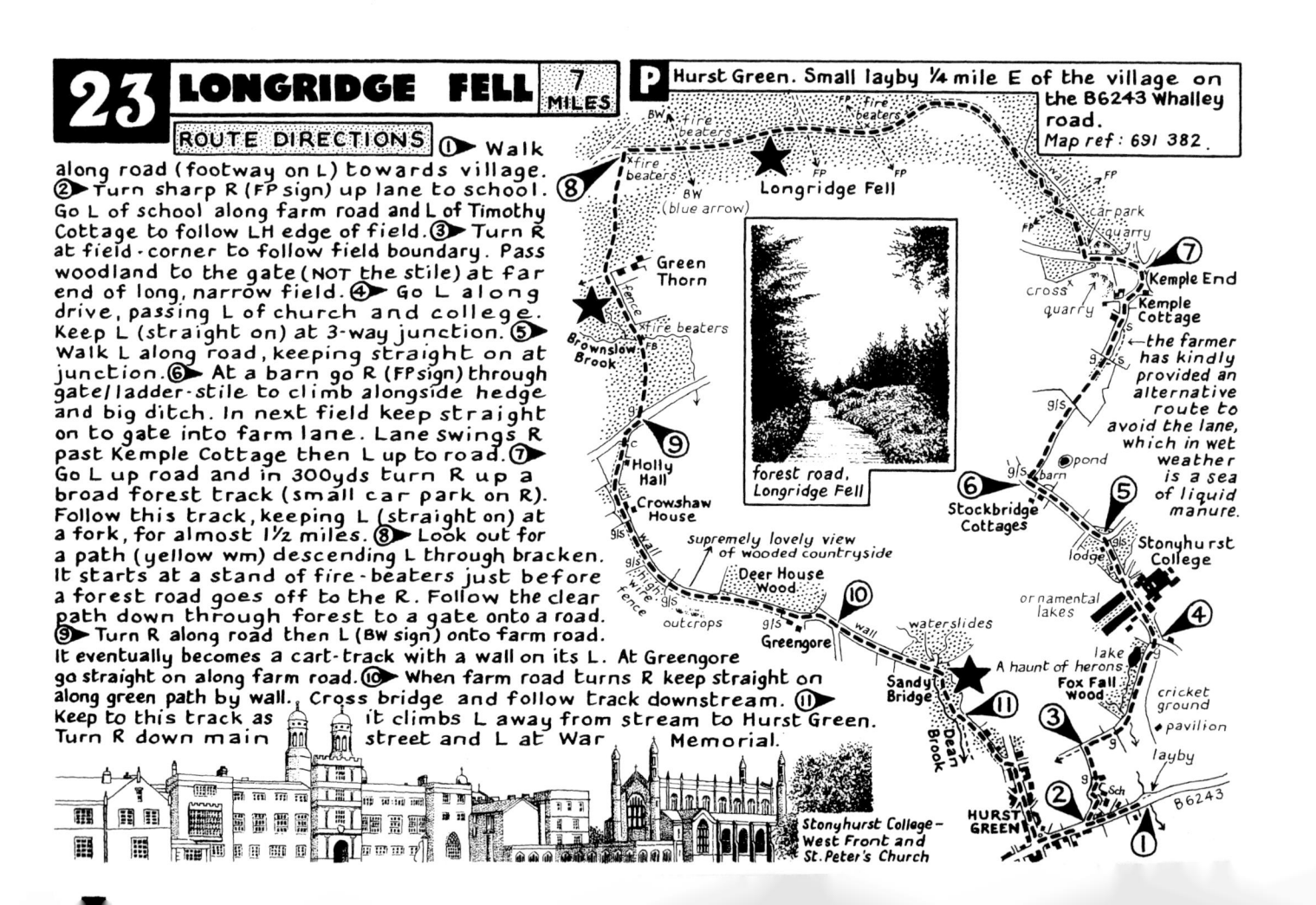

23 LONGRIDGE FELL 7 MILES

P Hurst Green. Small layby ¼ mile E of the village on the B6243 Whalley road. Map ref: 691 382.

ROUTE DIRECTIONS

①▶ Walk along road (footway on L) towards village. ②▶ Turn sharp R (FP sign) up lane to school. Go L of school along farm road and L of Timothy Cottage to follow LH edge of field. ③▶ Turn R at field-corner to follow field boundary. Pass woodland to the gate (NOT the stile) at far end of long, narrow field. ④▶ Go L along drive, passing L of church and college. Keep L (straight on) at 3-way junction. ⑤▶ Walk L along road, keeping straight on at junction. ⑥▶ At a barn go R (FP sign) through gate/ladder-stile to climb alongside hedge and big ditch. In next field keep straight on to gate into farm lane. Lane swings R past Kemple Cottage then L up to road. ⑦▶ Go L up road and in 300yds turn R up a broad forest track (small car park on R). Follow this track, keeping L (straight on) at a fork, for almost 1½ miles. ⑧▶ Look out for a path (yellow wm) descending L through bracken. It starts at a stand of fire-beaters just before a forest road goes off to the R. Follow the clear path down through forest to a gate onto a road. ⑨▶ Turn R along road then L (BW sign) onto farm road. It eventually becomes a cart-track with a wall on its L. At Greengore go straight on along farm road. ⑩▶ When farm road turns R keep straight on along green path by wall. Cross bridge and follow track downstream. ⑪▶ Keep to this track as it climbs L away from stream to Hurst Green. Turn R down main street and L at War Memorial.

forest road, Longridge Fell

Longridge Fell

Green Thorn

Brownslow Brook

Holly Hall

Crowshaw House

Deer House Wood

Greengore

supremely lovely view of wooded countryside

Sandy Bridge

Dean Brook

Kemple End

Kemple Cottage

— the farmer has kindly provided an alternative route to avoid the lane, which in wet weather is a sea of liquid manure.

Stockbridge Cottages

Stonyhurst College

ornamental lakes

Fox Fall wood

A haunt of herons

cricket ground

pavilion

layby

waterslides

HURST GREEN

B6243

Stonyhurst College — West Front and St. Peter's Church

Generally very easy walking, with one moderately strenuous section above Kemple End. Almost entirely on good tracks and paths. Only 1 ladder-stile (with adjacent gate). 1 mile on motor-roads (either with walkways or almost traffic-free). 2½ miles through forest and woodland. A walk abounding with *interesting* features through some of the *loveliest* countryside in the Ribble Valley - and that's saying a lot!

dovecote, Kemple End

STONYHURST COLLEGE

originally belonged to the Bayley family and later to the Shireburns. The heraldic devices represent these families - the eagle of the Bayleys and the lion of the Shireburns. In 1592 Sir Richard Shireburn began to build a new house here which was to remain the family home until the death of Sir Nicholas, the last Shireburn, in 1717. The mansion subsequently fell into disrepair, and in 1794 it was handed over to the Society of Jesuits. Stonyhurst has, since then, been considerably extended, and is now one of England's most eminent public schools. The many priceless treasures in the college museum include the embroidered cap of Sir Thomas More (1478-1535), Catherine of Aragon's religious robes and a cloak of Henry II's which was later worn by Henry VIII at the Field of the Cloth of Gold (1520). Much older than any of these, however, is the 7thC copy of St.John's Gospel - the oldest surviving English bound book. The magnificent West Front is flanked by the beautiful St.Peter's Church, built 1832-5 and modelled upon King's College Chapel, Cambridge. Some of Stonyhurst's famous ex-pupils are the poet Gerard Manley Hopkins (1844-89), Sir Arthur Conan Doyle (1859-1930), creator of Sherlock Holmes, and the actor Charles Laughton (1899-1962), immortalised as the cruel Captain Bligh in the memorable film 'Mutiny on the Bounty' (1935).

KEMPLE END is a

hamlet of very attractive farms and cottages. The old quarries, now colourfully bedecked with bilberry, heather and bracken, once provided the stone for the building of Stonyhurst. The small cross in a field up on the left is known as Paulinus Cross.

LONGRIDGE FELL is the most southerly named 'Fell' in the country. Its summit stands at 1148', but the highest point reached on this walk - point ⑧ - is 1024'. The extensive plantations consist mainly of sitka spruce, larch and lodgepole pine, and provide an ideal habitat for the shy roe deer. Birds to look out for are sparrowhawk, kestrel, short-eared owl and tawny owl.

GREENGORE is an ancient house remarkable for its massive buttresses. The present building - originally a shooting-lodge - dates from the 17thC., but it is on record that there was a house here in 1314, and Greengore is locally reputed to have been a hunting-lodge of King John (1199-1216)

SANDY BRIDGE is a delightful spot. Here Dean Brook - its banks fringed with ferns and foxgloves - cascades down through glorious beech woodland. Long ago men came here to dig the sand (hence the name) which they sold as floor-covering to poor folk who had no carpets or lino. There were once 4 water-powered bobbin mills along Dean Brook.

THE ALMSHOUSES at Hurst Green came from Kemple End, where they were built in 1706. In 1946 they were dismantled and reassembled on their present site. Note the stately semi-circular steps and the Shireburn arms.

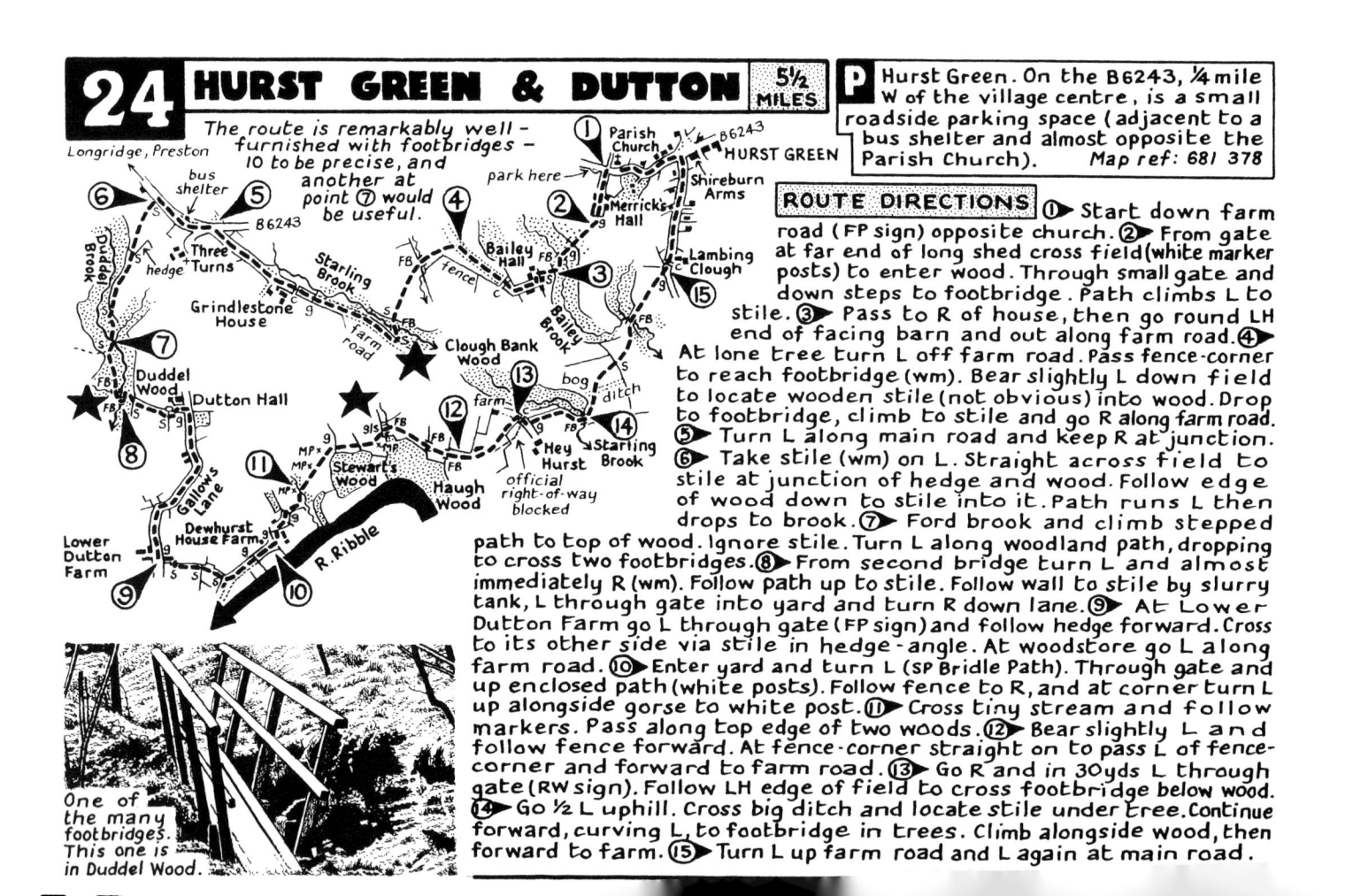

The route is remarkably well-furnished with footbridges — 10 to be precise, and another at point ⑦ would be useful.

Longridge, Preston

P Hurst Green. On the B6243, ¼ mile W of the village centre, is a small roadside parking space (adjacent to a bus shelter and almost opposite the Parish Church). Map ref: 681 378

ROUTE DIRECTIONS ①▶ Start down farm road (FP sign) opposite church. ②▶ From gate at far end of long shed cross field (white marker posts) to enter wood. Through small gate and down steps to footbridge. Path climbs L to stile. ③▶ Pass to R of house, then go round LH end of facing barn and out along farm road. ④▶ At lone tree turn L off farm road. Pass fence-corner to reach footbridge (wm). Bear slightly L down field to locate wooden stile (not obvious) into wood. Drop to footbridge, climb to stile and go R along farm road. ⑤▶ Turn L along main road and keep R at junction. ⑥▶ Take stile (wm) on L. Straight across field to stile at junction of hedge and wood. Follow edge of wood down to stile into it. Path runs L then drops to brook. ⑦▶ Ford brook and climb stepped path to top of wood. Ignore stile. Turn L along woodland path, dropping to cross two footbridges. ⑧▶ From second bridge turn L and almost immediately R (wm). Follow path up to stile. Follow wall to stile by slurry tank, L through gate into yard and turn R down lane. ⑨▶ At Lower Dutton Farm go L through gate (FP sign) and follow hedge forward. Cross to its other side via stile in hedge-angle. At woodstore go L along farm road. ⑩▶ Enter yard and turn L (SP Bridle Path). Through gate and up enclosed path (white posts). Follow fence to R, and at corner turn L up alongside gorse to white post. ⑪▶ Cross tiny stream and follow markers. Pass along top edge of two woods. ⑫▶ Bear slightly L and follow fence forward. At fence-corner straight on to pass L of fence-corner and forward to farm road. ⑬▶ Go R and in 30yds L through gate (RW sign). Follow LH edge of field to cross footbridge below wood. ⑭▶ Go ½ L uphill. Cross big ditch and locate stile under tree. Continue forward, curving L, to footbridge in trees. Climb alongside wood, then forward to farm. ⑮▶ Turn L up farm road and L again at main road.

One of the many footbridges. This one is in Duddel Wood.

Easy and mostly downhill as far as point ⑩; thereafter a little more strenuous. This is the Ribble Valley at its pastoral best, with glorious woodland, chuckling streams and exquisite views. No ladder-stiles. ¾ mile on motor-roads. For maximum enjoyment the walk should be done in DRY WEATHER. After prolonged rain the going becomes heavy across soggy pastures. NOTE: DUDDEL BROOK MUST BE FORDED AT POINT ⑦ – A TRICKY MANŒUVRE IF THE STREAM IS IN SPATE. To be on the safe side, pop a couple of plastic bin-liners into your rucksack.

MERRICK'S HALL

has a very long history, and was once a priest's residence serving the chapel at nearby Bailey Hall. The present building dates from the early 17th C., but was partially rebuilt in Georgian times. The name is that of a family who owned the farm in the 18th C.

BAILEY HALL

was built in the late 16th C. on the moated site of an earlier hall. Close by on its N side are the scant remains of the Chapel of St. John the Baptist, founded c1325 by Sir Robert de Cliderhoe. Tiny fragments of the N and E walls still stand, and there are steps (covered) down into a small crypt. The chapel's last worshippers bade farewell in 1548, and it was demolished in the 1830s.

DUDDEL WOOD

The names 'Duddel' and 'Dutton' are thought to derive from Dudda, an Anglo-Saxon chieftain. Here we follow the sprightly Duddel Brook as it gurgles merrily down through an enchantingly beautiful wooded ravine. In spring and summer Duddel Wood, with its wealth of ferns and flowers, is a botanist's Paradise. On sunny autumn days the colours are quite sensational – a riotous display of red, yellow, brown and gold. Look out for a weedy old mill pond and the fragmentary remains of a former bobbin mill.

DUTTON HALL

one of the finest old houses in the Ribble Valley, was built by Richard Towneley during the reign of Charles II. Its most striking feature is the splendid square central bay topped with a balustrade. Balconies such as this were a popular feature of 17th C. manor houses.

HURST GREEN

is not a particularly pretty village, but it contains much of interest, and is well-loved by Lancashire ramblers, for it lies amid some of the loveliest countryside in the county. For some notes on Stonyhurst College, the Almshouses and Dean Brook see Walk 23.

GALLOWS LANE owes its macabre name to the fact that a gibbet once stood in the vicinity of the road junction now known as **THREE TURNS**. The corpse of Ned King, a notorious local highwayman, dangled on public display from this gibbet after he had been tried and hanged for his crimes.

LOWER DUTTON COTTAGE (left) and **PEAR TREE COTTAGE** belong to a picturesque group of 17th C. buildings at point ⑨.

P Marles Wood Car Park, on the unclassified road between Ribchester Bridge and Old Langho. Car park is 1 mile E of bridge. Map ref: 675 356

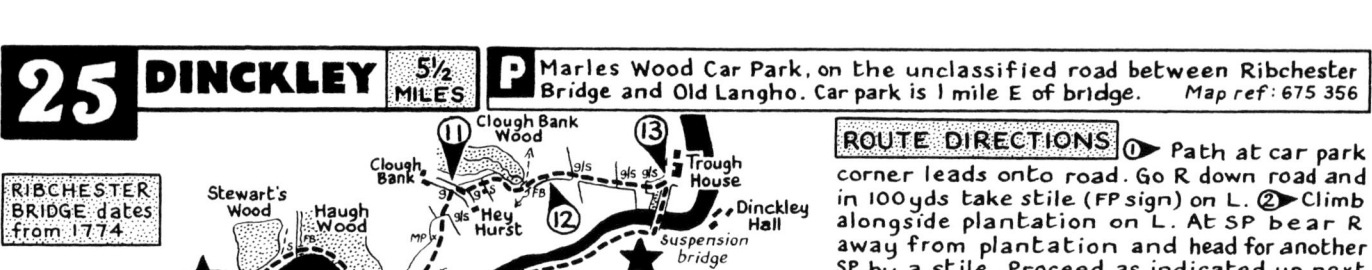

RIBCHESTER BRIDGE dates from 1774

The DE TABLEY INN is named after a local landowning family. Good ale here.

ROUTE DIRECTIONS

① Path at car park corner leads onto road. Go R down road and in 100yds take stile (FP sign) on L. ② Climb alongside plantation on L. At SP bear R away from plantation and head for another SP by a stile. Proceed as indicated up next field, crossing a cart-track to reach a pond. Turn R and follow fence on L. ③ Turn L (FP sign) along green track between hedges. Through farmyard to gate (wm) and straight on along farm road. ④ Immediately after passing a long row of cottages turn R down gravel road. ⑤ Pass through a gate then turn R over stile (wm) to go down RH side of field. Pass a pond and keep straight on over stile in wire fence. Keep to RH side of field to walk by wire fence down RH side of shallow ravine. ⑥ Look out for wm post on other side of ravine and cross to it. Climb with wire fence on L. Go past trough (old bath) to stile and continue forward past posh house on L. ⑦ Take RH of two metal gates (wm) and turn R to follow hedge, with ravine on L. When hedge turns away keep straight on past powerline pole to stile (wm). Turn L to gate/stile onto road. ⑧ Go R along road, cross bridge and turn R (RW sign) to follow farm road to Dewhurst House. ⑨ Enter yard and turn R (RW footpath) down path to ladder-stile. Turn L upstream. After passing below a wood, keep R down to footbridge and clear woodland path. ⑩ Leave wood at stile and turn L (RWsign) to climb steeply. When wood turns away L keep straight on over the hill. Pendle Hill and suspension bridge appear directly ahead. Make for gate/ladder-stile in crossfence, then keep near LH side of field, passing a RW sign, to gate/stile (wm) in far corner. Cross field to small gate (wm). ⑪ Cross drive to small gate (wm). Follow LH field boundary to footbridge below wood. ⑫ Straight on with hedge/fence on R. When fence turns away R keep straight on along track. ⑬ Just before reaching farm buildings turn sharp R down narrow path and cross suspension bridge. Turn R along obvious path downstream. Eventually path bears L and soon forks. Go L up steps (concessionary path) to car park.

Easy walking through pastures and woodland, both of which can be muddy after rain. The route is generally well-waymarked, but nevertheless pay careful attention to the route directions. ⅓ mile on a motor-road (with footway). 2 ladder-stiles (1 with adjacent gate). Superb river scenery. This, in the author's opinion, is one of the two most beautiful stretches of the Ribble. Which is the other? (Answer at foot of page).

25

MARLES WOOD

Marles Wood is better known as 'Sale Wheel Woods', and is an exceptionally popular local beauty spot. A remnant of the ancient woodlands which long ago covered most of this area, it is at its loveliest in May and June when the bluebells make a magnificent show. Breeding birds include Great Spotted Woodpecker (above left), Pied Flycatcher (above right), Spotted Flycatcher, Nuthatch, Treecreeper, Sparrowhawk and the raucous Jay.

SALE WHEEL
On reaching Marles Wood the Ribble enters a limestone gorge. The hitherto sedate river becomes a rushing torrent as it twists and corkscrews between huge, smooth, tilting slabs of rock, providing good sport for canoeists. On emerging from these narrow confines the water forms a whirlpool known as Sale Wheel.

Ribchester Bridge

Sale Wheel from Marles Wood

ALONG THE WAY WE ENCOUNTER SEVERAL SMALL **PONDS**, AND EACH IS A MICROCOSMIC WORLD TEEMING WITH WILDLIFE BENEATH, ON AND ABOVE THE WATER. YELLOW IRIS GROWS IN PROFUSION AROUND THEIR MARGINS, PROVIDING IDEAL COVER FOR MOORHENS, AND IRIDESCENT, BULBOUS-EYED DRAGONFLIES DART HITHER AND THITHER IN A FRENZIED SEARCH FOR PREY.

NOTABLE BUILDINGS

● **BOLTON HALL**, with its delightfully tipsy mullioned windows, is a splendid 17th C. manor house. ● **NEW HALL**, recently restored from a crumbling ruin, was built by George Talbot in 1665. Note the talbot (heraldic term for a dog) between the porch windows. ● **HEY HURST** is an attractive house built in Jacobean style. ● **DINCKLEY HALL**, seen away to the left from the suspension bridge, is one of the oldest houses in the Ribble Valley, dating from at least the 14th C. The Talbot family lived here until 1677, and it is reputed to have been a hiding place for Royalist forces during the Civil War (1642-51).

DINCKLEY FOOTBRIDGE, an impressive structure, was built to replace a boat ferry. A stone commemorates the official opening of the bridge on 10th October 1951. The ferry had been operated by the Trough House farmer, and anyone wishing to cross had to give him a shout. It is said that he was stone deaf until a boat load had gathered! The bridge was badly damaged by storms and floods in 1982.

Answer : The gorge between Gisburn and Sawley.

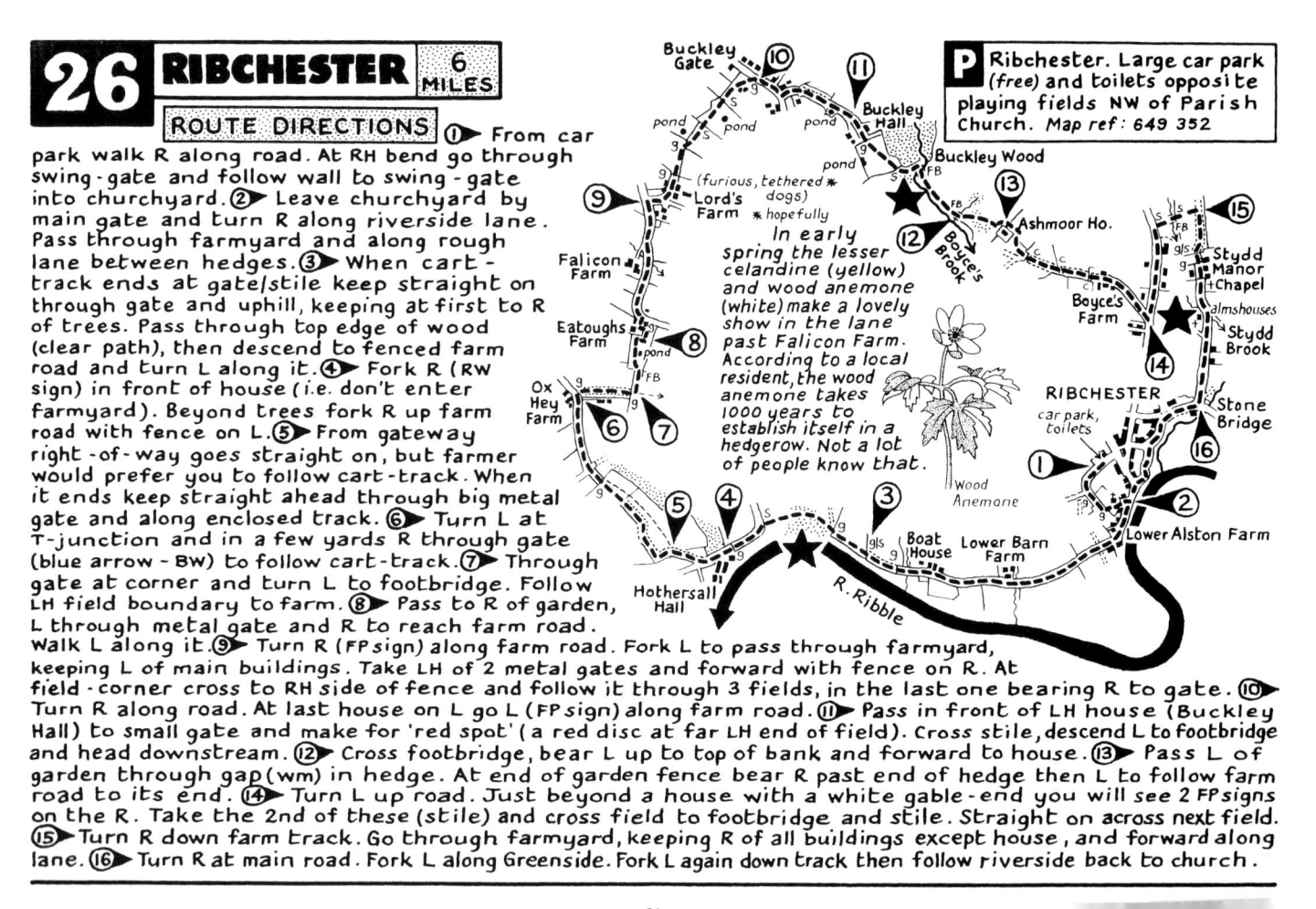

26 RIBCHESTER — 6 MILES

P Ribchester. Large car park (free) and toilets opposite playing fields NW of Parish Church. Map ref: 649 352

ROUTE DIRECTIONS

① From car park walk R along road. At RH bend go through swing-gate and follow wall to swing-gate into churchyard. ② Leave churchyard by main gate and turn R along riverside lane. Pass through farmyard and along rough lane between hedges. ③ When cart-track ends at gate/stile keep straight on through gate and uphill, keeping at first to R of trees. Pass through top edge of wood (clear path), then descend to fenced farm road and turn L along it. ④ Fork R (RW sign) in front of house (i.e. don't enter farmyard). Beyond trees fork R up farm road with fence on L. ⑤ From gateway right-of-way goes straight on, but farmer would prefer you to follow cart-track. When it ends keep straight ahead through big metal gate and along enclosed track. ⑥ Turn L at T-junction and in a few yards R through gate (blue arrow – BW) to follow cart-track. ⑦ Through gate at corner and turn L to footbridge. Follow LH field boundary to farm. ⑧ Pass to R of garden, L through metal gate and R to reach farm road. Walk L along it. ⑨ Turn R (FP sign) along farm road. Fork L to pass through farmyard, keeping L of main buildings. Take LH of 2 metal gates and forward with fence on R. At field-corner cross to RH side of fence and follow it through 3 fields, in the last one bearing R to gate. ⑩ Turn R along road. At last house on L go L (FP sign) along farm road. ⑪ Pass in front of LH house (Buckley Hall) to small gate and make for 'red spot' (a red disc at far LH end of field). Cross stile, descend L to footbridge and head downstream. ⑫ Cross footbridge, bear L up to top of bank and forward to house. ⑬ Pass L of garden through gap (wm) in hedge. At end of garden fence bear R past end of hedge then L to follow farm road to its end. ⑭ Turn L up road. Just beyond a house with a white gable-end you will see 2 FP signs on the R. Take the 2nd of these (stile) and cross field to footbridge and stile. Straight on across next field. ⑮ Turn R down farm track. Go through farmyard, keeping R of all buildings except house, and forward along lane. ⑯ Turn R at main road. Fork L along Greenside. Fork L again down track then follow riverside back to church.

In early spring the lesser celandine (yellow) and wood anemone (white) make a lovely show in the lane past Falicon Farm. According to a local resident, the wood anemone takes 1000 years to establish itself in a hedgerow. Not a lot of people know that.

Wood Anemone

(Map labels: Buckley Gate, Buckley Hall, Buckley Wood, Lord's Farm (furious, tethered dogs) (hopefully), Falicon Farm, Eatoughs Farm, Ox Hey Farm, Hothersall Hall, Boat House, Lower Barn Farm, R. Ribble, Boyce's Brook, Ashmoor Ho., Boyce's Farm, Stydd Manor & Chapel, Stydd Brook, almshouses, RIBCHESTER, car park toilets, Stone Bridge, Lower Alston Farm, pond, FB)

Mostly farm tracks and pastures. Easy walking with very gentle gradients, although after heavy rain you will encounter some of the most glutinous mud you've ever set foot in. 1 ladder-stile. ½ mile on motor-roads. There are many features of historical interest, and some delightful riverside and brookside scenery. Botanists will find much to enthuse over in spring and summer. The route is somewhat complex; pay careful attention to map and/or route directions, or you may never be seen again.

26

RIBCHESTER

In 79 AD the Romans built a fort here at the intersection of the major roads from the West Coast to York and from Manchester to Carlisle. Bremetonacum Veteranorum thus occupied a position of vital strategic importance, and for at least three centuries was the greatest Roman fortress in Lancashire. It is estimated to have covered about six acres of ground, and a large portion of the site now lies beneath the church and churchyard. The fort's name suggests that retired Roman soldiers were allowed to live here on a pension. Adjacent to the church is a Roman Museum containing many relics, and nearby is a Roman Bath House which was partially excavated in 1927. The porch of the White Bull pub is supported by Roman Doric pillars reputed to have once formed part of a temple. Following the withdrawal of Roman forces in the 5th C the fort was plundered and burnt by barbarous tribes. The Normans built a village here (recorded in the Domesday Book as 'Ribel Caster') only for Robert the Bruce and his marauding Scots to knock it down again.

The lovely church dates back to the 13th C. and is dedicated to St. Wilfrid, a 7th C. Archbishop of York. The wall painting of St. Christopher probably dates from the days when prayers were offered in church before crossing the nearby ford. A rector named Drogo was drowned whilst crossing in 1246. There is a splendid Jacobean oak pulpit (1636), and a hole in the north wall of the chancel was possibly a hagioscope, or 'leper's squint'. The unusual dormer windows were added in 1712. The c 1700 churchyard sundial is inscribed 'I am a shadow. So art thou. I mark time. Dost thou?'

Stydd

OUR WALK THROUGH THIS HISTORIC HAMLET TAKES US PAST TWO BUILDINGS OF PARTICULAR INTEREST. THE TINY **ST. SAVIOUR'S CHAPEL** WAS BUILT IN 1136 BY THE KNIGHTS HOSPITALLERS, AN ORDER OF CRUSADING KNIGHTS WHO HAD TAKEN RELIGIOUS VOWS. IN THE GRAVEYARD IS THE BASE OF AN

Stydd Almshouses

ANCIENT CROSS. A LITTLE FURTHER ALONG THE LANE WE COME TO THE QUAINT, ITALIANATE **ALMSHOUSES**, BUILT BY THE SHIREBURNS OF STONYHURST IN 1726 FOR 'FIVE CATHOLIC LADIES, WIDOWS OR SPINSTERS'. IT IS AN UTTERLY CHARMING BUILDING AND IS STILL IN USE, HAVING BEEN MODERNISED IN 1962 AND AGAIN IN 1990.

BOAT HOUSE

A ferry across to Osbaldeston Hall is known to have existed as long ago as 1355

HOTHERSALL HALL stands on the site of a much older house. It was rebuilt in 1856 by one Jonathan Openshaw, a rich woollen manufacturer from Bury.

ornamental lamp post, Lord's Farm. Dogs under control here, please.

Boat House (visited on Walk 26)

Osbaldeston Hall

R. Ribble

Dobridding Wood

lone tree

pond

Mercyfield Wood

Nightfield Gate

ruined barn

Pewter Cottage

barn

Smalley Fold

trough

pond

The 'lone tree' at point ⑪

hollow

pond

tennis court

Oxendale Hall

rough lane

pond

Osbaldeston Green

Robert's House Farm

Osbaldeston Lane

Commons Lane

Bay Horse

A59

FP Mellor

Farm road

fence fence

The CORMORANT, a coastal bird, makes occasional forays up the Ribble.

P Osbaldeston. Locate the Bay Horse pub on the A59 (Map ref: 647 317) and take the lane opposite. In 100 yds you will find on the R, by a FP sign, a small parking space for no more than two cars.

Note: Maria and Steve, at the Bay Horse, are happy for walkers to use their car park. Nevertheless, it would be courteous to ask permission.

ROUTE DIRECTIONS

① From Bay Horse walk W (towards Preston) along main road. ② Immediately past garage take stile on R and follow RH edge of field. ③ R along lane then L along Commons Lane. ④ Take stile (FP sign) on R and follow shallow ditch across field to footbridge. Follow LH edge of field to cross stile in hedge and continue forward. ⑤ Go L through gate/stile and follow hedge on L. On reaching pond use metal gate to cross to other side of hedge. ⑥ Pass to R of all farm buildings and on to distant barn. Through gate to R of it and pass LH end of house to stile. ⑦ Turn L and immediately L again along narrow tarmac lane. ⑧ At next house go R through gate. Bear slightly L across field to stile in hedge. Forward alongside broken hedge. Keep L of pond and straight on through two hedge stiles. ⑨ R along lane. ⑩ Just past woodland where lane bends L go R through gate/stile (FP sign) and down two fields to stile into wood. Path drops to footbridge then climbs to leave wood at kissing-gate. ⑪ Cross field, passing lone tree, to join an old cart-track. Follow it round to R then turn sharp L down another cart-track. Follow riverside path upstream. ⑫ Don't use gate/stile in crossfence. Instead turn L across tiny stream to stile. Continue upstream until deflected R by fence/ditch. ⑬ Through metal gate and forward with fence on R. At field-corner go L with fence. ⑭ At crossfence take LH of two gates. ⑮ Go R through gate into farmyard, then R between buildings and out along farm-road. Just as it starts to climb more steeply turn L through gate to green track between fences. Cart-track continues between trees then swings R up to gate at fence-corner. ⑯ Turn L to stile into wood. Slippery path drops to stream then

Pastures, woodland, riverbank and lanes. Fairly easy walking, but two or three steep and very slippery woodland paths. No ladder-stiles. 1 mile on motor-roads -- virtually traffic-free apart from 200yds of the A59.

27

climbs to stile. Walk up middle of field. Pass L of small hollow, through gap in crossfence, L of pond then head for stile at LH corner of field. ⑰▶ Drop to footbridge and climb to stile. Cross field to stile immediately L of tennis-court then straight on along gravel drive. ⑱▶ At lane go R for a few yards then L (SP Roberts House Farm). Follow LH field boundary. Pass between two barns then R along a farm road. ⑲▶ L along lane and L again at Y-junction (SP Whalley).

Osbaldeston

A peaceful rural parish made up largely of scattered farms, lush pastures and beautiful woodlands sweeping steeply down to the south banks of the Ribble. Here are several important historic houses and some highly desirable modern residences - they're not short o' brass on Osbaldeston Lane. The BAY HORSE, which began life as a farm, has been an inn since about 1825.

● NIGHTFIELD GATE IS DATED 1747

OSBALDESTON HALL

, A HOUSE OF MANY GABLES, WAS FOR SEVERAL HUNDRED YEARS — UNTIL THE MID 18TH C ~ THE ANCESTRAL HOME OF THE OSBALDESTON FAMILY, AND WAS ORIGINALLY BUILT WITH STONE FROM RIBCHESTER'S ROMAN RUINS. THE HOUSE WAS REBUILT IN THE EARLY YEARS OF THE 17TH C, BUT STILL RETAINS AN ELIZABETHAN DOORHEAD DATED 1593. THE OSBALDESTONS OWNED A FERRY ACROSS THE RIBBLE WHICH IS KNOWN TO HAVE BEEN IN USE AS LONG AGO AS 1355; THE BOAT HOUSE CAN BE SEEN ACROSS THE RIVER. THERE WAS A SPOT OF BOTHER AT THE HALL IN 1606 WHEN THOMAS OSBALDESTON TOOK A DISLIKE TO HIS SISTER ELIZABETH'S BRIDEGROOM, ONE EDWARD WALSH, AND SLEW HIM IN A DUEL. THE GHOST OF POOR OLD ED IS SAID TO ROAM THE HOUSE, MOANING AND EXPOSING A GAPING CHEST WOUND.

Little Commons   Osbaldeston

OXENDALE HALL

This noble house, now delightfully restored, was built by Lawrence Osbaldeston in 1656. In December 1940 an 8' long land mine was found hanging by parachute from a tree near the house. It remained suspended for 3 days before being exploded by the Naval Bomb Disposal Squad. Several windows were shattered by the blast, but no serious damage was done.

28 LONGRIDGE & KNOWLE GREEN · 5½ MILES

P Longridge. Car park and toilets at the E side of town in King Street adjacent to Longridge Health Centre. Map ref: 606 373

Note: This car park is very small and soon fills. There are other car parks (pay and display and a bit pricey) in the town centre off Berry Lane.

ROUTE DIRECTIONS

① (See NOTE on next page) Walk up road, passing to L of White Bull. In about ½ mile fork R. ② Where road bends L go R (FP Knowl (sic) Green) over stile by huge, ugly iron gates and along cart-track. In 170 yards go through stone stile and forward with wall on R. At next gate path becomes enclosed. ③ Through gate and L along tarmac lane (but first go straight on for 30 yards to inspect Written Stone). Straight through Cottam House farmyard and down cart-track, soon forking R down grassy path with tiny stream on L. ④ Turn L along road. ⑤ Just past 'Knowle Green' sign turn R along a lane. Keep straight on (R at all junctions), then R down steps to cross footbridge. Follow clear path downstream. ⑥ At stone gateposts turn L down steps, past barn and L down lane. ⑦ Cross ford. A few yards ahead is another ford, but DON'T cross it. Instead turn L into a narrow path between gardens to a gate. Forward for 100 yards, R over footbridge then L to follow stream. ⑧ Turn R up lane. In 50 yards go R (FP sign) over stile and ½ L up field to gate at top RH corner. Forward to road. ⑨ Go L a few yards then R through gate (FP sign). Bear R to RH field boundary and follow it to farm. Straight through yard, R along lane and R at T-junction. ⑩ Turn L (FP sign) along track to Haven Farm. Pass L of house and down walled track. ⑪ At bottom turn R (wm) up track through trees, then cross two fields to gate at far RH corner. ⑫ Don't use gate, but turn R over stile and cross field to far RH corner. Go round RH side of small wood and forward along cart-track. Cross road and straight on (FP sign) along farm road. ⑬ Just before house turn R (wm) to iron stile, then L to another. ½ R across field, through gateway in fence, then L towards trees. Cross footbridge and straight on to reach gate to L of farm

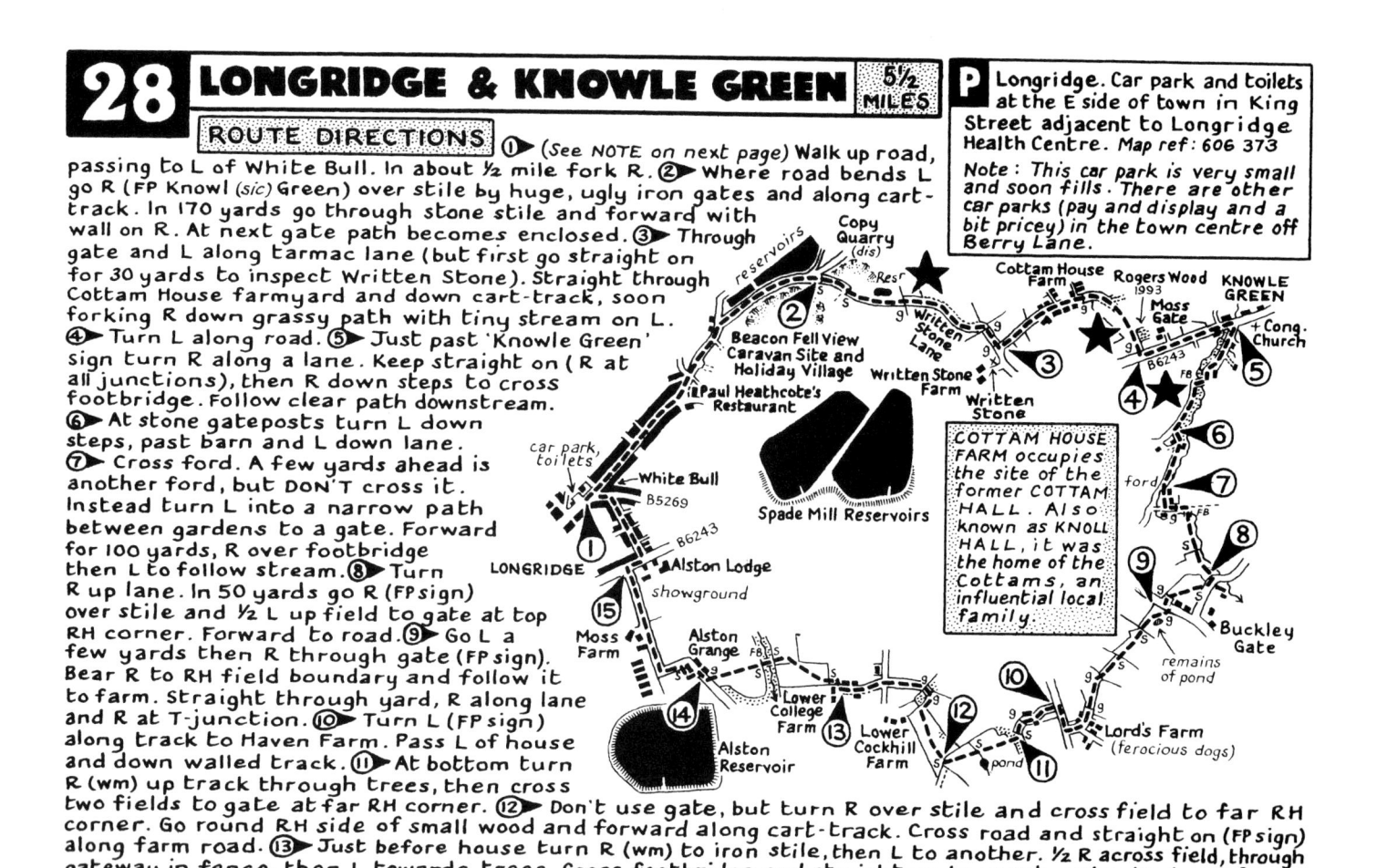

COTTAM HOUSE FARM occupies the site of the former COTTAM HALL. Also known as KNOLL HALL, it was the home of the Cottams, an influential local family.

Easy going, but can be abominably muddy in places, so best done after a long dry spell. As far as point ⑦ the walk is on good tracks and paths, with fine views of the Ribble Valley and a lovely woodland section. Thereafter it is mostly pathless pastures as far as Alston Grange. 1¼ miles on motor-roads (nearly all with footway). Only 2 (small, iron) ladder-stiles, but not a particularly good walk for dogs because of livestock in the fields. Beware of huge bulls and savage farmyard dogs, both of which can seriously damage your health.

NOTE: The extensive area of old quarries to the NE of Longridge is now largely occupied by a caravan park. The right-of-way shown on the O.S. map, starting at Paul Heathcote's Restaurant and winding through this area, via Tootle Height, to Green Banks, has become impassable; in fact it's no longer findable. Regrettably, therefore, this walk must now begin with a somewhat lengthy uphill tarmac trudge. To rub salt into the wound, notices at the park entrances insist that people refrain from walking dogs through the site.

buildings. ⑭▶ Turn R along farm road but don't go through yard. Instead turn L and pass around back of buildings to stile back onto farm road. ⑮▶ Turn R along main road, take first road on L, and at top turn L to White Bull.

LONGRIDGE

owes its growth to the Industrial Revolution. By the early 1800s hand spinning and weaving were well-established cottage industries. Stone quarries around Tootle Height began to operate in 1830, and 1840 saw the opening of a railway, for horse-drawn trains, from the quarries to Preston. The introduction of steam locomotion in 1848 led to the building of 4 mills, and between 1851-81 the population trebled. High railway charges killed the prosperity of the quarries, and the line closed in 1967. All the mills closed down between 1935-64. Longridge, however, remains the shopping and social centre of the local farming area, with an excellent range of facilities.

KNOWLE GREEN

A quiet hamlet set amidst beautiful rolling countryside. The thriving little Congregational Church was built in 1866. From here we follow Cowley Brook down a lovely wooded glen, passing *en route* the remains of several old bobbin mills.

The strange heads on the porch of Haven Farm. Origin unknown.

Haven Farm used to be called 'Hades'.

THE WRITTEN STONE

RAUFFE·RADCLIFFE·LAID·THIS
STONE·TO·LYE·FOR·EVER·A·D·1655

It is thought that this 8' long stone was placed here by Ralph Radcliffe following four deaths in his family within a short space of time – probably due to plague. The passing years have seen the 'WRITTEN STONE' become the subject of many local legends, one of which tells us that a farmer once moved the stone into his dairy. It was to serve as a utensil stand, but any pots or pans placed upon it would shake, spill or topple off. When milk churns were stood on it the milk immediately turned sour. The poor farmer soon decided to return the stone to its original resting place.

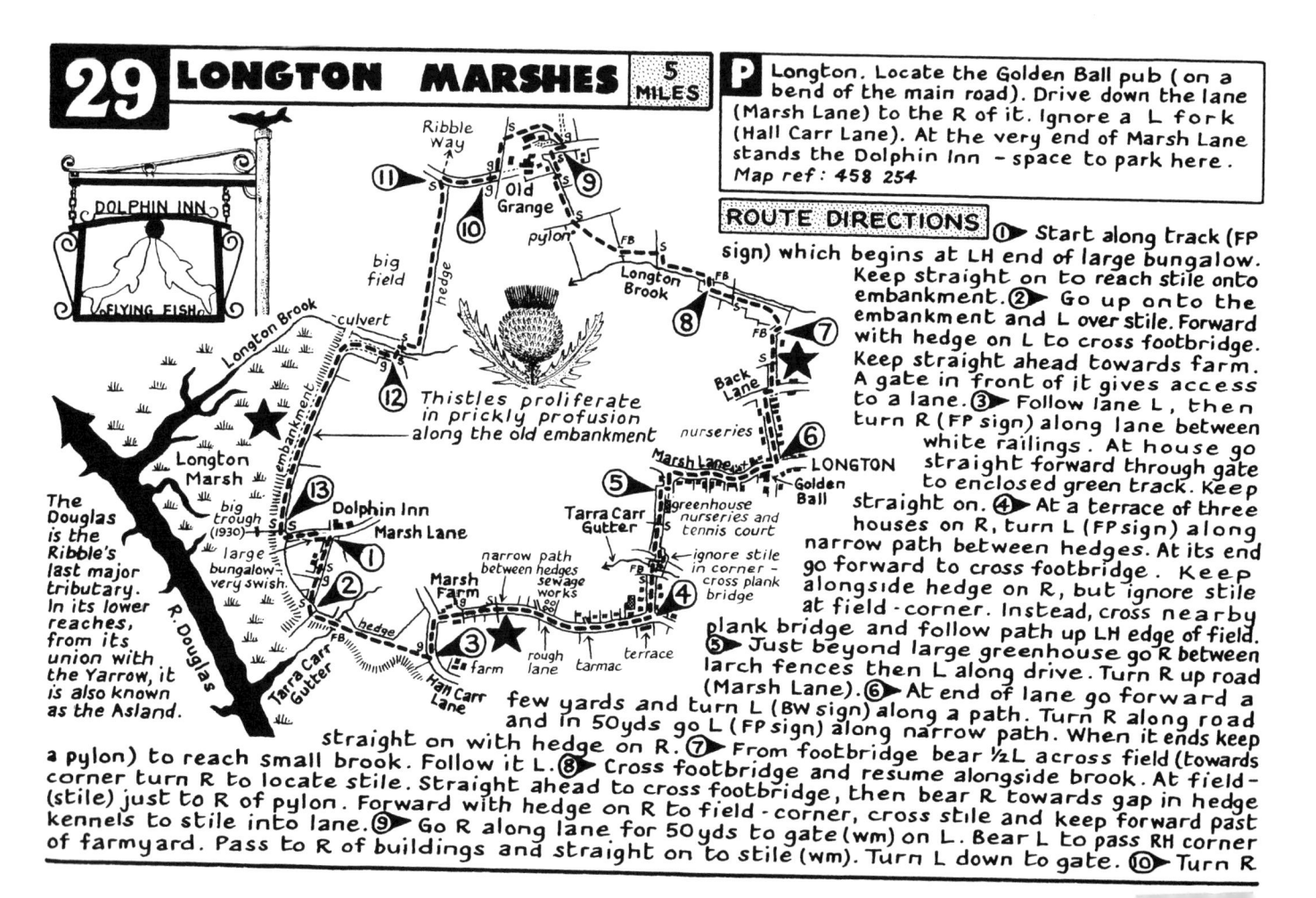

P Longton. Locate the Golden Ball pub (on a bend of the main road). Drive down the lane (Marsh Lane) to the R of it. Ignore a L fork (Hall Carr Lane). At the very end of Marsh Lane stands the Dolphin Inn – space to park here. Map ref : 458 254

ROUTE DIRECTIONS

① Start along track (FP sign) which begins at LH end of large bungalow. Keep straight on to reach stile onto embankment. ② Go up onto the embankment and L over stile. Forward with hedge on L to cross footbridge. Keep straight ahead towards farm. A gate in front of it gives access to a lane. ③ Follow lane L, then turn R (FP sign) along lane between white railings. At house go straight forward through gate to enclosed green track. Keep straight on. ④ At a terrace of three houses on R, turn L (FP sign) along narrow path between hedges. At its end go forward to cross footbridge. Keep alongside hedge on R, but ignore stile at field-corner. Instead, cross nearby plank bridge and follow path up LH edge of field. ⑤ Just beyond large greenhouse go R between larch fences then L along drive. Turn R up road (Marsh Lane). ⑥ At end of lane go forward a few yards and turn L (BW sign) along a path. Turn R along road (FP sign) along narrow path. When it ends keep straight on with hedge on R. ⑦ From footbridge bear ½L across field (towards a pylon) to reach small brook. Follow it L. ⑧ Cross footbridge and resume alongside brook. At field-corner turn R to locate stile. Straight ahead to cross footbridge, then bear R towards gap in hedge (stile) just to R of pylon. Forward with hedge on R to field-corner, cross stile and keep forward past kennels to stile into lane. ⑨ Go R along lane for 50yds to gate (wm) on L. Bear L to pass RH corner of farmyard. Pass to R of buildings and straight on to stile (wm). Turn L down to gate. ⑩ Turn R

Thistles proliferate in prickly profusion along the old embankment

The Douglas is the Ribble's last major tributary. In its lower reaches, from its union with the Yarrow, it is also known as the Asland.

Easy, level walking; absolutely no hills whatsoever. The varied terrain includes quiet lanes, enclosed paths, pathless pastures and grassy embankments. Only 1/3 of a mile on motor-roads. 4 ladder-stiles (1 with adjacent gate). Nobody will die of excitement on this walk, but nonetheless it's an interesting expedition in that it presents a quite startling contrast between the bustle of modern suburbia and the utter tranquillity of the lonely, windswept marshes.

along farm road. ⑪► Turn L over ladder-stile (SP Ribble Way Footpath) and follow LH hedge across huge field. Near end of field turn R (RW sign). In 60 yds go L (RW sign) to cross brook via two ladder-stiles. ⑫► Turn R through gate and along cart-track. At RW sign track swings L to run along embankment. ⑬► Over stile (big trough on R) and turn L to lane back to Dolphin.

THE DOLPHIN

In the late 1830s this was a private house belonging to a local brewer. (As you walk up Marsh Lane you will notice, on the R, a modern housing development called 'The Maltings'. This was the site of the brewery, which ceased production in the 1950s) The tidal waters must have practically washed the brewer's doorstep; remains of the original embankment can be seen running across the fields from the Dolphin to Longton Brook. The Dolphin is known to have been a pub since 1881. Don't be discouraged by its outward appearance, which is unprepossessing to say the least. Step inside and enjoy a noggin in an attractive and well-appointed lounge which was once a boathouse. Cheers!

The Dolphin Inn is generally regarded as the official starting point of the RIBBLE WAY, a 70 mile long footpath to the river's source high on the fells of the Yorkshire Dales (see P 11). The possibility of creating such a route was first mooted by the Preston and Fylde group of the Ramblers Association in 1967. There followed many years of wrangling over rights-of-way, and it was not until a Ribble Way Committee was formed in 1980 that any real progress was made. By 1985 an official route as far as Gisburn had been established, and on 1st June that year the opening ceremony was performed at Edisford Bridge. A route beyond Gisburn was devised by Gladys Sellers; and her guidebook, 'The Ribble Way', was published by Cicerone Press.

The attractive Park Farm at the top of Marsh Lane

LONGTON

An ancient village once described as one of the prettiest in Lancashire, and in days gone by famed for its gooseberries. Longton has also, at various times, produced bricks, beer and baskets. By-passed in the 1950s, the village continues to prosper, with modern, affluent-looking housing estates intermingling with nurseries, market-gardens and smallholdings.

THE MARSHES

FOR CENTURIES THE TIDAL FLATS HAVE BEEN PROGRESSIVELY ENCLOSED, AND THE LAND RECLAIMED, BY THE BUILDING OF EARTH EMBANKMENTS. THE ONE WE WALK ALONG TODAY WAS CONSTRUCTED IN THE 1850s. IN AUTUMN AND WINTER THE MARSHES ATTRACT MASSIVE FLOCKS OF WADERS AND WILDFOWL. THERE ARE OFTEN LARGE NUMBERS OF WHOOPER SWANS AND THE SMALLER BEWICK'S SWANS. THESE DIFFER FROM THE MUTE SWAN IN HAVING A BLACK, 'KNOBLESS' BILL WITH A YELLOW BASE. THE MUTE SWAN'S BILL IS ORANGE.

Mute Swan

Whooper Swan

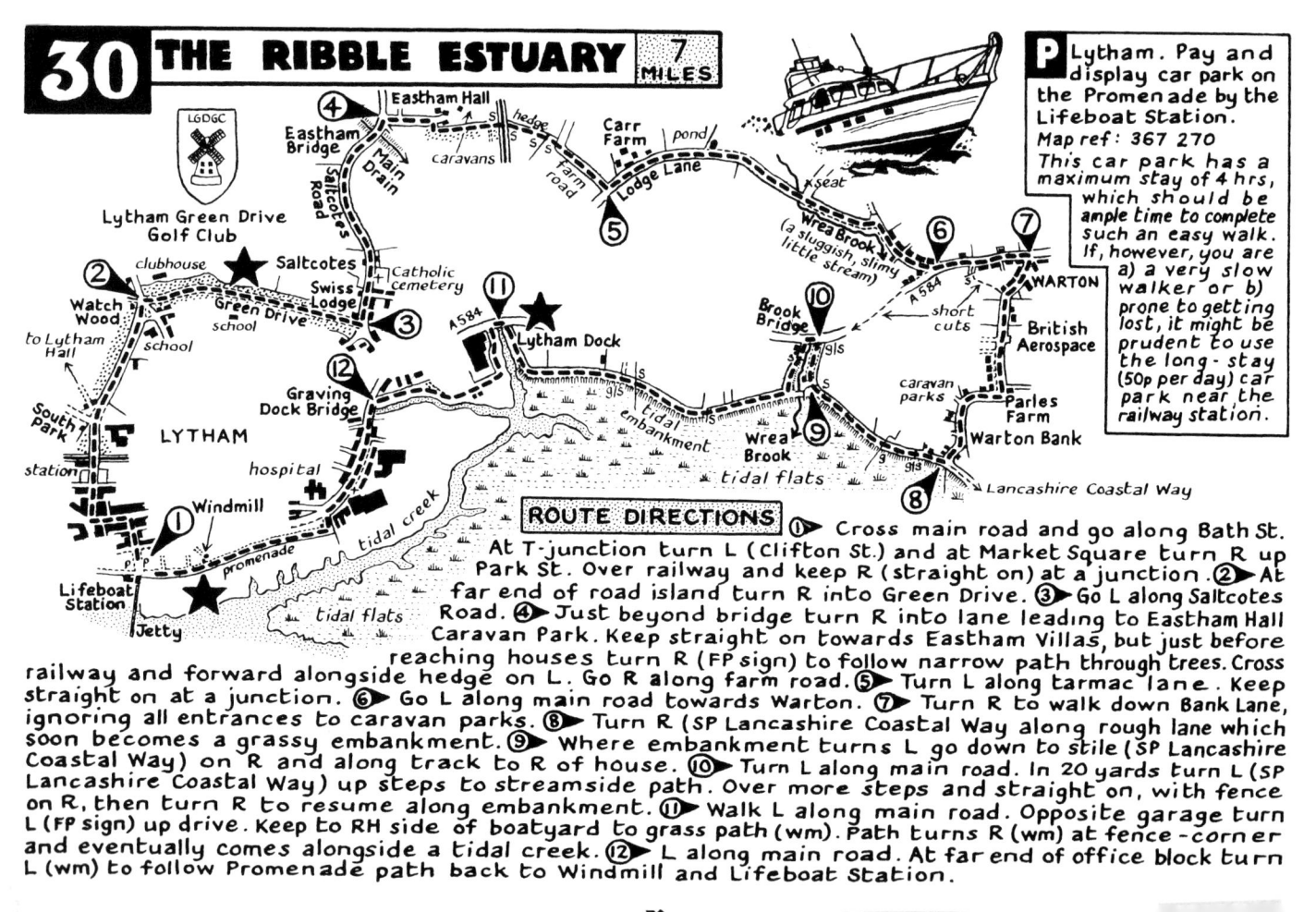

30 THE RIBBLE ESTUARY · 7 MILES

P Lytham. Pay and display car park on the Promenade by the Lifeboat Station. Map ref: 367 270 This car park has a maximum stay of 4 hrs, which should be ample time to complete such an easy walk. If, however, you are a) a very slow walker or b) prone to getting lost, it might be prudent to use the long-stay (50p per day) car park near the railway station.

ROUTE DIRECTIONS

① Cross main road and go along Bath St. At T-junction turn L (Clifton St.) and at Market Square turn R up Park St. Over railway and keep R (straight on) at a junction. ② At far end of road island turn R into Green Drive. ③ Go L along Saltcotes Road. ④ Just beyond bridge turn R into lane leading to Eastham Hall Caravan Park. Keep straight on towards Eastham Villas, but just before reaching houses turn R (FP sign) to follow narrow path through trees. Cross railway and forward alongside hedge on L. Go R along farm road. ⑤ Turn L along tarmac lane. Keep straight on at a junction. ⑥ Go L along main road towards Warton. ⑦ Turn R to walk down Bank Lane, ignoring all entrances to caravan parks. ⑧ Turn R (SP Lancashire Coastal Way along rough lane which soon becomes a grassy embankment. ⑨ Where embankment turns L go down to stile (SP Lancashire Coastal Way) on R and along track to R of house. ⑩ Turn L along main road. In 20 yards turn L (SP Lancashire Coastal Way) up steps to streamside path. Over more steps and straight on, with fence on R, then turn R to resume along embankment. ⑪ Walk L along main road. Opposite garage turn L (FP sign) up drive. Keep to RH side of boatyard to grass path (wm). Path turns R (wm) at fence-corner and eventually comes alongside a tidal creek. ⑫ L along main road. At far end of office block turn L (wm) to follow Promenade path back to Windmill and Lifeboat Station.

Dead-flat and dead-easy. The outward route, as far as point ⑧, is almost entirely on tarmac. Henceforth the walk follows the well-waymarked route of the Lancashire Coastal Way, reaching Lytham Docks after a 1½ mile stroll along the grassy tidal embankment. I small ladder-stile. 1¾ miles on motor-roads with pavements, 1½ miles on quiet lanes. The walk, which will particularly appeal to birdwatchers and boat freaks, has a profusion of interesting features — but it's a far cry from Penyghent!

LYTHAM

Originally a Saxon settlement, and recorded as 'Lidum' in the Domesday Book, Lytham was but a small town until fairly recent times, and owes its development to social changes brought about by the Industrial Revolution.

The coming of the railway in 1846 saw holidaymakers arriving in droves from Lancashire's rapidly growing mill towns, yet Lytham has remained a genteel, dignified resort, with none of the brashness of neighbouring Blackpool. Along its tree-lined streets you will find high-quality shops and restaurants interspersed with elegant Georgian town houses. The grandest house of all is Lytham Hall, built in 1757-64 on the site of a 12th C Benedictine priory, but the grounds are private and we shall see only the entrance gateway.

WARTON

This village is famous for its association with aircraft. During the last war Warton was a large Base Air Depot receiving new planes from America and modifying them for operational use. Today the huge British Aerospace complex is one of the country's leading centres for the design and production of military aircraft.

LYTHAM DOCK

CONSTRUCTED 1840-2, AND BUSY FOR HALF-A-CENTURY UNTIL THE OPENING OF PRESTON DOCKS TOOK AWAY TRADE AND LYTHAM TURNED TO BOATBUILDING — CHIEFLY RIVERBOATS FOR AFRICA. THIS INDUSTRY CEASED IN 1955, AND THE DOCKS NOW PROVIDE ANCHORAGE AND REPAIR SERVICES FOR LOCAL CRAFT

- **LYTHAM GREEN DRIVE** is one of 4 fine local golf courses. The others are FAIRHAVEN, ST. ANNE'S OLD LINKS and the famous ROYAL LYTHAM AND ST. ANNE'S, venue of many Open Championships.
- *SWISS LODGE, a most striking house at the end of Green Drive, was built in 1864 in memory of one of the Clifton family.*

Lytham has boasted a windmill for at least 800 years. The present one was built in 1805, and operated until 2nd January 1919, when it was gutted by fire. Open to the public (free entry) and simply MUST be visited; the imaginative displays and exhibitions are superb. Be sure also to visit the adjacent, and equally fascinating, Lifeboat Museum.

Note: The drawing depicts the windmill as it was prior to Christmas Eve 1997, when a ferocious storm destroyed the sails.

THE ESTUARY, a National Nature Reserve, is Britain's third most important for waders. Birds of this type regularly seen are oystercatcher, dunlin, knot, black-tailed godwit, sanderling and redshank. Various birds of prey, including our smallest hawk, the merlin, frequent these marshes, whilst in winter there are often large flocks of lapwing, golden plover and brambling.

Oystercatcher

Black-tailed Godwit

PLEASE OBSERVE THE **COUNTRY CODE**

- Enjoy the countryside and respect its life and work
- Use gates and stiles to cross walls and fences
- Keep your dog under close control
- Protect wildlife, plants and trees
- Help to keep all water clean
- Make no unnecessary noise
- Fasten all gates

- Leave livestock, crops and machinery alone
- Keep to public paths across farmland
- Take special care on country roads
- Guard against all risk of fire
- Leave no litter